The Book of
Daily Channeled Messages

By
Dyan Garris

www.voiceoftheangels.com
www.newagecd.com

Journeymakers, Inc.

The Book of
Daily Channeled Messages

By
Dyan Garris

www.voiceoftheangels.com
www.newagecd.com

Journeymakers, Inc.

© 2007 Dyan Garris
All Rights Reserved,
including the right of reproduction
in whole or in part in any form.

Published in the United States of America.
No part of this book may be used or reproduced
in any manner whatsoever without the written
permission of the publisher.

Cover art by Limebar Creative

ISBN: 978-0-9776140-8-0

Printed in the United States of America
10 9 8 7 6 5 4 3 2 1

TABLE OF CONTENTS

The Book Of
Daily Channeled Messages

How To Use This Book

The Book of Daily Channeled Messages is a compilation of angelic channeled messages from a one year period of time. These messages post daily on my website: www.voiceoftheangels.com.

There is more than one way to use this book. You can simply read it in order or open it to a random page when you feel you need angelic guidance.

Another way is to employ the technique of bibliomancy, sometimes referred to as libromancy. To use the book in this way, close your eyes, focus on your question or concern and open the book to a random page. With your eyes still closed, take your finger and point to a passage. Open your eyes and read what you are pointing to. This is your wisdom for the day.

Magic

It is one thing to have a key in your possession and quite another to actually insert it into a lock and use it to open something. It is one thing to see a rainbow, yet another to go and get the gold that we know is there at the end. Both require effort. And it is helpful to still believe in magic.

Your Painting

Peel off layers of fear and doubt. Shed these things like old clothes that are worn out, no longer fit or have gone out of style. Cover yourself not with heavy blankets of protection, which can actually suffocate you when wrapped too tightly; but live your life rather like unclothed magnificence that ventures out into the fresh air. Release weight and release patterns. Restore your painting. It is a masterpiece waiting patiently to be unveiled.

Where is Your Balloon?

Let's say that more than anything, you want to manifest a relationship. Take a balloon and tether it to a string. Then fill it with helium and write the word "Relationship" on it. Tie it securely to your ring finger and try to go about your day. You now have a relationship. Now try to get dressed.

As part of manifesting, we must let go of things, rather than hold on to them too tightly. To do so hampers our progress. We must let go so that these things can fly as high as they need to. Depending on your thought process patterns, you may expect the balloon to return to you as a deflated piece of rubber. That is possible if you, (a) keep it tied to your finger for a long period of time, and (b) fool yourself into thinking you are releasing it; but you release it into the confined space of a particular room in your house.

However, also depending on your thought process, you may know that once you let it go where it needs to go, say up to the heavens, it returns in a different form, and probably not as a deflated piece of rubber that hits you in the face on its way back to you.

So now you have a choice between the need to control and trust in the transformation process. Where is your balloon?

More on Manifesting and Balloons

You can apply this balloon imagery and principle of manifestation to any aspect of your life. It doesn't just apply to relationships. Whatever you are trying to manifest, intentions must first be set. Get a firm picture of your desires in your mind. Then write whatever it is you think you want on the balloon. And again, tie it to your finger for a while. You will notice that after a while having the thing tied to your finger may get in your way. So, at the appropriate time, be willing to let it go completely. Trust.

To hang on limits the way this returns to you. You don't want it to return as a balloon, do you? You want what you *wrote* on the balloon to manifest.

Before you let it go, it is just what it is – a thought, a desire, written on something you are attached to. It is by letting it go and giving it freedom to fly that you give it the opportunity to transform.

Once you let go completely, do not be attached to the outcome. Do not go flying around looking for the balloon. Do not try to follow the balloon into the sky or attempt to control where it goes. Do not give the balloon instructions on how to get where it is going or what it is supposed to do when it gets there.

Allow whatever you have manifested – put forth in thought, word and action – to come back to you, not as a flat one or two-dimensional concept, but as true form.

The Party

Everyone in your past, present, and future is and was an invited guest in your drama. You invited them to come into your life and teach you something about love, even if it doesn't or didn't feel that way. It is the truth. We must take total responsibility for the guest list, otherwise we become like a child whose illicit party got out of hand and now expects someone else to clean it up. As adults, realize you can have the party; but everyone there is a guest – an honored guest – and you alone are responsible for cleanup. Honor your connections. All of them. Forgive those whom you perceive have wounded you. Anything that is not love is an illusion. To do otherwise is to keep yourself locked out of your own celebration. The party then becomes a bitter pity party of one, rather than a joyful reunion.

Sabotage

You get invited to a picnic and are asked to bring something. You decide you will bring a sandwich. As you prepare the sandwich, your poverty consciousness (that is the consciousness that tells you that you don't have enough) kicks in and you decide that you can only afford to bring one half of a sandwich. So that is what you do.

On the way there you eat half of the sandwich yourself because you feel entitled to do so. When you get there no one wants to share it with you; and you tell yourself that your sandwich must somehow be inferior, all the while thinking to yourself that you made it with good intentions. So you do not understand what the problem is.

While you are talking about yourself to someone, the sandwich falls to the ground and ants become interested in it. You tell yourself that this sort of thing always happens to you and you do not know why.

What you are missing is that if you were paying attention, if you were not so self focused, if you covered the sandwich or made sure it was in a place where it wouldn't fall carelessly to the ground, you would still have it and be able to enjoy it or share its enjoyment with others, even though it is only one half of what it could be. This is self sabotage.

Crawl?

Here are the reasons we do not empower ourselves: (1) We feel entitled; (2) We feel wounded; (3) We feel entitled to be wounded. All are illusions of the ego-self.

The only ones who are entitled to anything are helpless infants. As a child, first you crawled, then you walked, then you fell. Someone either picked you back up so you could try again, or you figured out how to get up yourself and try again. Eventually you walked. If you refuse to walk you relegate yourself to a life of crawling around on the floor focusing on dirt, lint, and other basic debris that probably doesn't even belong to you and/ or that you did not create.

In order to move forward you must first walk and that entails perhaps picking oneself up, dusting oneself off, bandaging what appears wounded, and realizing that you are all grown up and entitled to nothing. You were given a fabulous opportunity for life and the tools with which to shape it in any fashion you desire. Live it!

 **The Coin**

Imagine that a coin sits on a table and has been there for years. If the table is made of dense wood, how does one see the other side of the coin? How does one even know there is another side? After a while, one might even stop noticing that the coin is even there, let alone wonder anything about it. You could flip it over, but then the flip side is in darkness as well. And, it might not even occur to you to flip it over.

If you expand your mind a bit, it might occur to you to slide it over to a glass table. This would be a parallel shift. Then in order to see the other side without picking it up, one would actually have to crawl under the table to do so. This, of course, would take some possibly contortionistic effort.

Such it is when attempting to see the other side of something in a linear fashion. It's when you discover with glee that you can actually pick the coin up, go out the door, and actually purchase something with it, that you have discovered/encountered the power of self-transformation and self-empowerment.

So, instead of staring blindly at your coin or moving it to the left or right, or exerting great, and perhaps pointless effort in attempting to see the other side, simply pick it up, walk out the door and enjoy.

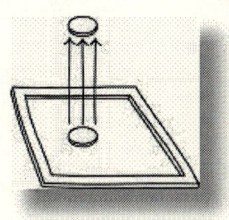

Home

The ideal "home" is one in which the caretakers empower their children with their own abilities and skills for survival, rather than feeding their childlike desire to be fed. In this way, someday, if and when they return home, they return not as little children but as adults, bringing with them the fruits of their labors.

Extra Baggage

Energy and matter come together whenever they are supposed to for whatever reason they are supposed to. Let things unfold in your life instead of trying to control everything.

This only blocks the flow. In any relationship from the past, be it parent-child, business, love relationship, in-laws, or other, honor the person that came into your life to help you with your lessons. Honor the work that you did together. Honor the results. Then instead of carrying bitterness around with you like unnecessary luggage, bless them, release them and send whatever bad feelings you still have around them or the situation up and away. This frees up your creative energy. It unblocks you so you can move forward. It allows you to be able to manifest in an unrestricted manner.

Those of you that think you've already done this, you must do it in spirit as well. Do it from a meditative state. This speaks to the person's spirit and it frees you both. The other choice is to lug the heavy pack around with you wherever you go. You might find it rather cumbersome as you swim in crystal clear, uncharted waters.

The Truth Is

Sometimes it is easier to fool ourselves into believing what we believe to be true, rather than face the real truth. Sometimes facing the truth would mean that we would have to change. No one likes to be wrong, and this is why we find change so challenging. What if facing the truth did not mean that you were wrong, but simply meant that the truth was true?

To shift to this perspective one would have to let go of ego attachments and set their intentions to live in the truth, no matter how that shows up.

You will know when you are ready to live in the truth when your old patterns no longer serve you and you are not attached to being wrong or being right. The truth lies outside of those concepts. It simply IS.

Sink or Swim

You can't control the waves in the ocean, but you can ride them if you so dare. Life is a bit like the ocean. You either figure out how to ride the waves, with or without a board, and roll with them, instead of against them – without getting smashed or drowning – or in the alternative, you can just sit on the beach and remark to yourself how lovely they are. It is your choice.

Waiting

It seems as if we're always waiting for something. . .waiting in line, waiting for our check, waiting for so and so to call, waiting to start fresh, waiting, waiting, waiting. Why have we put ourselves in jail like this? Release yourself and let go of your "if only's." There is no waiting. Consider doing something constructive with the wait time. Live.

The Wall

When you find a brick wall in your face, you still have some choices.

You can have a tantrum. You can try to break through. You can turn around and go back into the past. You can wait until it dissolves. Trust that the wall is there for a reason, even if you can't see what that is.

While you're there, do another thing. Release. Releasing is not the same as giving up. Releasing is letting go of your attachment to outcome. So do that. You might find, as well, then, that the wall is something of your own creation. Are you perhaps in your own way?

Little

When you're little, learning to walk can seem like an impossible challenge. Then you develop enough to just be able to do it and soon it becomes second nature. You never think about how to actually do it after that.

Then at some point you start learning to talk; and in order to read and write, you need to learn the basis of that – you need to learn your ABC's. You need to learn foundations and structure.

Eventually you learn to solve for X. Imagine trying to solve for X when you don't yet know the alphabet. The two may seem unrelated – letters and numbers – but they aren't. These are foundational concepts for higher learning. So it is with spiritual growth. Little by little you start to see. And then, a big growth spurt is possible. Take little steps before you attempt to run the marathon.

Spiritual Growth

Spiritual growth is much like physical growth. You don't wake up one morning being at your full height. It just takes time to grow and develop. Embrace every stage. When cleaning your spiritual house, don't expect growth and transformation to occur all at once. Clean your spiritual house room by room and corner by corner and soon you will see tangible progress.

The Soul's Journey

When we blame someone for wounding us, we are in our own way. When we are angry with someone, we are in our own way. When we stubbornly refuse to see, we are in our own way. When we insist on staying in patterns that were taught to us, we are in our own away. As adults, we must take responsibility for our choices and respect the choices of others.

We all have a journey. It is all a lesson in Love. If you realized that you had pre-planned your journey, your challenges, people you would meet, circumstances you would face – if you realized you set this all up for yourself – could you at that point begin to forgive? Would you begin to see how freeing that knowledge could be? It would certainly give you a whole new perspective. It takes some courage to face the truth; because once you have it, you can't go back.

 **Reverse Gear**

So you go to work and at some point you collect a paycheck. In most cases this could be construed as a fair exchange of energy. That's fine. However, if you perceive that this is the only way things are and that this is the only way things will ever be and that is just how things show up in the world, you have just effectively limited yourself.

You have limited all other ways of fair exchange entering your life for the "work" that you do.

There are no limitations if you open your mind to infinite possibilities, rather than having tunnel vision of the way things are "supposed" to show up. By your thought process you have manifested things showing up this way and therefore they do.

Ditto for relationships. If you expect persons to show up a certain way and/ or at a certain time, you limit yourself for things showing up differently. You block the flow of synchronicity.

Open yourself to the possibility that you are the one creating blocks and limitations in your life. If you want to change things, simply reverse the process by which you created what you have now. Shift gears and see the road from a whole different perspective. You may find while you are driving backward that you are really going forward at the same time. Open your mind.

Perspective

So many are afraid to love. What doesn't make sense about this is that it is like saying that you aren't going to walk because you might fall down. So you crawl instead, thinking that you are safe down there crawling around on the floor. What you do not realize is that you can still bump your head on the table leg.

Designer Labels

One of the first things one asks upon meeting someone new is, "What do you do?" We then apply the answer to a frame of reference that we have in our minds – an existing belief system – as to what the answer means. From there, we draw certain conclusions based upon what we think we know and/or what we think we see or perceive.

If we didn't have these physical bodies as a boundary, if our system wasn't built on pieces of paper as measures of status and credentials, we would be able to see a person's soul. We could look far beyond what we think we see or the way things appear to be. Upon meeting, we then might ask, "Who are you?"

We would then perhaps recognize and embrace with all our heart a person that we already know, if we could just see through the illusion. If you can, try to expand your mind and consciousness to the place where there are no limitations and let go of the need for labels. They only really serve designers.

Dorothy

If you are harboring anger toward someone, this is in your way of self-empowerment. You are giving your power away to this situation. Ditto for harboring resentment on any level, avoidance, and denial. Self-empowerment and subsequent transformation comes from realizing you have a choice.

You cannot change anyone else's mind, behavior or actions. To attempt to do so is a waste of your time and energy. What we really want when we are angry with someone is for him or her to validate us and validate our feelings about whatever it is we perceive was done to us by them. You have the power to validate yourself.

Like Dorothy in *The Wizard of Oz*, the power was there all along. She had to (1) become aware that she even had the ruby red slippers on and (2) figure out how to use them to get where she wanted go. From there, it was all really simple, wasn't it?

Unless you need the grand adventure, there is no sense in keeping yourself in the illusion. She was right when she said there is no place like home. However the question always remains – who would she be without that very interesting journey? People empower themselves when they are ready.

You Can

We don't come into our incarnations
disliking ourselves. We come in with
our crown chakras open and we come
in trusting and loving and completely
accepting of self. We learn self-loathing,
patterns of abuse, self-doubt and fear
along the way; and usually we learn this
from someone else. This is where you
gave your power away. These aren't
your patterns. They are someone else's.
Return to the light. Return to liking
yourself and believing that you can do
anything, because you can.

The Plan

Do not bemoan a lack of talent in a
particular area of your life. Do not
be envious of someone else's gifts.
Appreciate them instead. This is honoring
of the Creator and the light in all of us.

Take all of your own special talents and gifts and use them at their highest level. Develop and nurture those talents that you do have, like a special garden that you have planted with care. This path will ultimately lead you to where you need to be. It is when you make peace with yourself and allow yourself to open and blossom, like a unique flower, that you begin to see synchronicity and meaning in your life. Let the plan reveal itself by getting out of your own way.

High Beams

In the big scheme of things, we are here for such a short span of time. We do get to choose what we will learn. Sometimes that learning may take an entire lifetime. Sometimes we don't see the big picture until the very end. Yet sometimes, we have that blazing moment of clarity when everything finally makes total sense. It is what we do with that moment that matters. This is the space where miracles occur.

But nothing can occur if you are blocking that space. Free yourself from your previous viewpoints that have kept you stuck in endless cycles and patterns. If you can grasp the concepts of the repetitive patterns in your life, if you can get to the root of the matter, if you can for one moment step outside of your stubborn ego position, you may be able to truly understand your role in your own drama. From there, perhaps you will be able to clearly see other people's roles, as well.

Open your mind to the possibility that the anger, hurt, resentment, fear, and belief systems that you hold on to so tightly keep you from the happiness that you say you want. It is not because of another person's actions that you are wherever you are. It is your choice. Try to see through the fog. Turning on your fog lights will help. Shine a bright light into the shadows and murkiness and what happens? You may just see things in a whole different light.

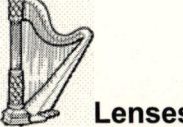

Lenses

You go to the store with your friend and try on different sunglasses. You try different colors and shapes. Note how things in the store look completely different depending upon which lens you are filtering the world through. You each buy a different pair.

While you are in the store, it rains and then clears up. You put your respective glasses on and exit the store. There is an awesome rainbow in the sky. One of you does not see it.

You take the glasses off and switch with your friend because you would like to share this vision. Now neither of you sees it because the moment of light has passed. However, when you were switching glasses, you suddenly noticed that your friend has blue eyes, not brown.

What we each see depends upon what we are looking at, through, from what angle, and when. What color are your lenses?

The Eye of the Storm

When one is in the eye of a storm, that force feels, seems, and looks to be destructive. However, the flip side of that is that it creates an environment and opportunity for cleansing, clearing, healing and rebuilding. It depends on how you look at it and through what eye you see with. In any situation, simply open your eyes and look beyond what you think you see. Therein lies the truth if you care to see it. Use your eyes.

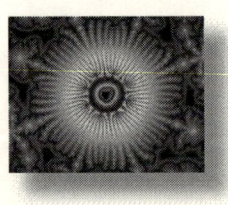

The Glasses

It is our illusions and distortions in perception about a situation, person, or event that keep us locked in repetitive patterns. Once those go, we can see clearly instead of looking through fuzzy lenses. The illusions are necessary to growth and learning. However, once they are stripped away completely, we can see clearly enough to make great strides on the path. If you like it fine where you are, then continue to try to see out of the same pair of old glasses. However, consider cleaning the lenses once in a while. It's a better view.

Great Strides

Whatever you do not take in stride will come back to walk or stand in front of you at one point or another.

Patterns and Integration

Patterns get integrated into the energy field and begin resonating as truth. This is why, if you want to change something, you must start with changing the pattern. Whenever a new pattern gets fully integrated into the field, it will begin resonating as the truth. Those of you with physical ailments, please note. Your body is doing what your mind has taken in as truth.

Study whatever it is that started the pattern. Get to the root of the thought patterns, physical patterns, which created such as truth for you. Eliminating the pattern allows shifts to take place and makes room for new patterns to filter in, thus instigating a change in what your physical body accepts as truth.

This is why something as simple as finding a new route to get somewhere will eventually begin to become as natural as the old way. The new pattern replaces the old. This begins to open up a whole new vista. Try it and see.

Once you integrate the concept, you can begin to easily make any changes you desire. It may take some courage to try a new way of doing something because fear is a pattern too. But if you are sincere in your desire to effect a change, eliminating old patterns and creating new is the basis of the facilitation of that.

 **Where Are You?**

Patterns can be good and helpful. A pattern of notes can make a beautiful melody. A pattern or routine can form a basis for intimacy and bonding. However, it is when a pattern is no longer conducive to growth that one finds the universe presenting them with opportunities for change. This can seem challenging or even scary to many.

Consider the following: You have a routine and a pattern and route that you use to go to work every day. It's comfortable. You don't think about it. You just do it and it takes you where you want to go. It's such a familiar route that you don't really even see what's around you anymore.

One day someone asks you for directions to your place of work and you are completely dumbfounded because you realize you don't know how to tell someone how to get there. You long ago stopped looking at street names. You just go there on autopilot.

The next day you find that the route you regularly take is under construction. This challenges you to find a different pathway. There are a few different ways of looking at this. You can grumble, complain, and resist change. Or you can keep an open mind and look at the whole thing as an exciting new adventure. What is your pattern?

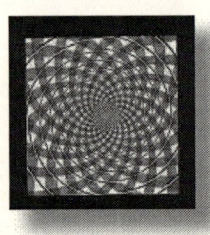

Right and Left

It is when we cling stubbornly to our point of view that we block our forward progress. Is it possible that you're wrong? Are we so attached to being right? Try looking left instead. There is a different view from over there. Insistence and attachment to being right limits all of the other directions your life might take. If you go back and take a fresh look at something you haven't looked at in a while, you might find that you never really saw it clearly to begin with. You might now see other things that you never noticed before. The attachment to being right is the ego's way of approval seeking, and not being right does not necessarily mean that you're wrong.

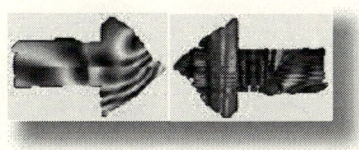

Valuable Consideration

Money is pieces of paper. Money is used as an exchange of energy. This could just as well be beads, corn, or in economic terms, guns and butter. The power that we perceive money to have is exactly that – a perception. And therefore, this is what gives it energy. It is under-"lying" belief systems that shape perception.

If you can start looking at money as energy, you can start opening channels to allow the flow of money into your life. Those that have perceptions of money as self-worth should seriously consider when they first started being a piece of paper.

Ascension

As you travel on your healing journey, ask yourself just where you are trying to go. We often think if we just have enough money or the right car or clothes, or whatever that this will bring happiness. Then we might be surprised to find that these things did not bring true joy. They are not tools for transformation. They are illusory and transitory playthings on the road from childhood to maturity.

If you continue to hold fast to your old patterns, you will still find them with you when you attain your version of "success." And those patterns will keep repeating and continue to be a theme in your life until you transform the core patterns – that is the patterns at the root.

There is a tendency to view change as "death." This is not so. Transformation leads to ascension; and ascension is where we find true joy, free from previous illusions and patterns. Ascension is not death. It is life. It is that which is risen and that which flies high and free. Imagine the view from up there!

The Bus

Why do we resist change so much? It is because of patterns. Sometimes it is easier to stay in our patterns than to try a new one. But in order to make a new pattern, change we must. So around and around we go. And that is a pattern too. Start small and change one thing in your routine or in your thinking. Soon, the old pattern goes and the new feels comfortable. Try to enjoy your process of transformation. It can be exciting.

Too often our focus is not on what we are doing but on everything else we have to do. Do you remember being sixteen and wanting to drive just for the sheer pleasure of driving? How many of you feel the same way about driving now? Change is part of life. Enjoy every minute of it. And if you don't, the choice is always there to take the bus instead.

Value

Sometimes we want something so much for so long and then when we get it we find it to be meaningless or not what we thought we wanted. It becomes passé after a while. Everything on this earth plane is perception and perspective. Everything is illusion, except Love. If you believe something to have value, then it does. If you believe that you have value, then you do. You do not need anyone else to deem you valuable. You just are.

A Different Beat

We are creatures of habit. Habits and patterns help us feel in control. And if we are in control, then we must be safe – or so our minds tell us. The challenge is to do something different, and this entails stepping a little out of our comfort zone. If we can manage this, we open the doors to positive change. We open the pathways to whatever it is we are trying to attract. We must get out of our own way and allow things to flow.

The universe has its own habits and patterns as well; and when we try to superimpose our own wills upon this universal will, this is when we have challenges in our lives. Life starts looking like unmerged layers in a computer graphics or photo program. Then we ask why. That is why. You are blocking the universe. Step aside and align your will with universal will and watch what happens. It may be a different beat than what you are used to, but you might find it easier to dance to.

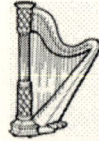 **Memory**

In any relationship that is sadly gone from your life, what you really are mourning is the feeling you once had. While you cannot go backward, cannot replace that particular feeling or that particular energy that existed between you at that particular time, you can move forward. To do this, start by honoring the exchange of energy that once existed. Thank, bless, and release and hold those memories close to your heart.

Like one of those beds that remembers and conforms to your body contours, memory is an interesting thing. It is not only in your mind, but exists on a cellular level, as well. So know that in some ways the person is always part of you. And cherish those memories.

Shampoo

How many of you have used the same kind of shampoo and conditioner for the last twenty years? Seems ludicrous, doesn't it? But this is how patterns are. Lather, rinse, repeat. Is this the story of your life? Sometimes if you just change one or two small things, it sets the stage for big change that could be easy and effortless, like buying and trying new shampoo. The power to change your life lies in the ability to change the underlying old pattern. Use the new shampoo to wash it all away. Condition and get new body. No need to repeat.

Hearts and Minds

We do not love with our heads. We love with our hearts. If you are trying to make a relationship decision based on what your linear mind tells you, then you will attract a person to engage in linear lessons with, rather than the love of your life. But the linear mind has its purpose. Decide with the linear mind to open the heart.

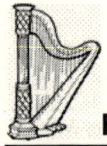

Foundation

Unconditional love has no agenda. It exists without manipulation or coercion. If you truly love someone, do let him or her go. Give them the freedom to learn, grow, discover and integrate higher learning. And in their absence, you do the same. Use your time wisely. If they make their way back to you, you have a solid framework to move forward with.

 **The Remote**

Along with the gift of every day comes a bonus item. It is the gift of possibilities and opportunities, however remote they may seem. When do you truly see this? Do you see this at the end of your life, or now, when you have the opportunity to be grateful for and appreciate all that you have – even if it is as simple as being grateful for the gift of breath?

Resources are finite and we all take them for granted. You get to choose how you will use your personal resources; but like small children who become bored with their toys, we have forgotten how precious our resources really are. It is only when the toy is broken or is taken away that one remembers the joy associated with it and then longs to have it back.

Choose either to stay embroiled in petty squabbles, like chickens, or choose to heal the root of your core issues so you can truly live, love, laugh, freely create and feel happiness and joy. Choose to listen, watch, or vibrate to any station or frequency you desire. As an adult, you are the person in charge of the remote, the station and the programming.

White Noise

When faced with a situation that seems hopeless, therein lies an opportunity for faith and therefore new hope. The key is to simply let go. Once you do that, hope is able to spring forth anew. If you are blocking the path with your own ego-based wants, needs and desires, perspectives and dictates, nothing can get through except static. You cannot clearly hear, see, feel, or perceive truth and guidance through the roar of the noise and distortion you are creating. Let go so the picture can become clear once again.

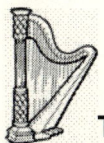

The Eagle

The eagle cannot soar if it has ice on its wings. Sometimes help is needed to deice. Warmth is what melts ice. And while the process of being temporarily constrained while the ice is melting can feel uncomfortable, it is necessary if one is to ever fly high and free again. It would be helpful to try to enjoy the warmth, instead of struggling against it.

When the ice melts, it turns into water. Water cleans, clears, and washes things away. Let someone help you with transformation of ice into water today, so you can reach the heights that you are capable of reaching.

Outside the Box

How do we learn? We learn by repetition or by experience or by repetition of experience. This is how learning becomes ingrained pattern. How do we unlearn, or create or transform, then?

Firmly set your intention for something new. Then take actual steps to shift and change the old patterns. That means you actually have to do something other than what you've always done. Take a chance and step outside of the box. It is the first step toward manifesting and it's a whole new world out there.

Just Be

The ocean knows what to do. It ebbs. It flows. It has moods. It goes in and out. It doesn't ask why. It doesn't ask how. Look at your personal journey in the same way. Go with the flow. It is such a simple phrase, but how do we do that exactly? BE the ocean. Sometimes you're stirred up. Sometimes you're calm, warm, and accepting. But the entire time you are flowing, healing, cleansing and most importantly, full of life. Just BE.

"The ocean can be moody, but full of life then too. Let the healing power that's there now gently enter you."
© Dyan Garris 1993 - 2007. *Voice of the Angels – A Healing Journey Spiritual Cards, The Ocean* card.

The Bigger Picture

One way to define "the bigger picture" is by trying to understand how everything weaves together. There is nothing we do that doesn't affect others. We are not living in our own little bubble. Everything has an effect. It is like ripples in a stream. They resonate out from their own center and have an effect on the entire body of water. We are all connected.

Another way to look at this is as a photograph. If the focus is on you, the bigger picture (the rest of what is in the photograph) becomes blurred and distorted and fades into the background. To be whole, one must have one's entire individual picture in focus.

Now, take a snapshot of everyone in your sphere and put them all together in a collage. Then you have at least part of the bigger picture. Take this concept and expand exponentially, and there you have the complete picture. Once you have that one-dimensional concept, you can then make a movie. And we all know that there is something very magical about the big screen.

Wrong Way?

Often we are faced with a choice or crossroads. Should we go left, should we go right, should we just not go at all or should we go another time or day? The answer is that there is no wrong answer. If you go left you will have certain experiences and meet certain people and certain things will happen. It is the same if you go right, even though it may appear different. The reason for this is because even though you will meet different people the lessons are the same. If you decide not to go, the lessons will still appear at some point. You will learn exactly what you are supposed to learn.

If you go a different day or way, it is the same thing. It is all about the lessons. So, when choosing, keep this in mind. There is no wrong choice. Everything weaves together the way it is supposed to.

The Future

Form follows thought. What you think about is what you create. So, now you think you're going along thinking and creating with positive thoughts and intentions, but everything seems like it is the same as it has ever been. Why haven't things changed and when will they?

First of all, realize that you probably spent a lot of time – perhaps even a lifetime – manifesting negatively. Now, in the present, you are simply living what you created in the past. This will take some time to clear. The good news is that it won't take a lifetime to clear. You can uncreate pretty quickly. From this moment on, focus on creating a different way. The key is in the patterns.

One of the reasons people don't change is because it is easier to continue on with ingrained patterns because they are familiar, even if they are unhealthy or unproductive. There is a certain illusion of comfort and safety. Prepare to enjoy your future. The future lies in the now.

Amnesia

The human capacity for love is so deep that it cannot easily be expressed by mere words. We are wired to love deeply and be loved as well. Love is all that is. However, it is an illusion to think that someone else can complete us. To believe so is to remain in a victim mode. We must first complete ourselves. We must each come to the party already whole.

Sometimes it happens that we feel an instant and very intense connection with someone. It could be someone we don't even really know. Our hearts leap in joy at this connection. It is very real and stays with us forever. This is soul mate connection. It is unmistakable. It is intense. This is simply recognition on a cellular level between two people. It is love remembered.

It is important to note that we can have more than one soul mate in our lifetimes. Soul mates often incarnate in the same lifetime – for however long or short of a period of time – as remembrance to the lessons that were previously signed up for. We do not necessarily end up with our soul mate as a life partner. It is simply about remembrance of who we are and what we came to do. A soul mate can show up in a brief way to remind us of our true path.

Every interaction between people, however subtle or brief, always has meaning. Study then where you are not whole. Make yourself whole. Give yourself love in everything you do. Get back on the path. Don't give your power away. It is not necessary to be a victim.

Honor that part of yourself that came home to greet you and remind you of self-love, however briefly or however long it lasts. No part of you is truly missing, even if it seems so. You are already whole, loved, and complete. You just temporarily forgot.

Ageless

When you were five years old, were you worried and fretting about being fifty-five? Probably not. You were probably busy daydreaming, playing, creating, building and living completely in the moment.

Do you have some kind of guarantee that you are going to live to be a ripe old age? Life is short and more precious than you know. Does it really take a near death experience to teach you that? Try being fully in every minute. Then the next time someone asks how old you are you can tell the truth.

Unconditional Love

We all want the same thing, to be loved, accepted, understood. Why does this seem so difficult to find or achieve? Well, it really isn't if you understand that you must first love yourself unconditionally and accept and understand yourself completely.

No one can give you this. You must first give it to yourself. Then you already have it and don't need someone to give it to you. You cannot go into any relationship thinking, "This is the person that is going to give me love." Go in already having this for yourself.

Bigger Ego

I can guarantee you that if you are at odds with someone you are in your ego and they in theirs. You cannot imagine how wonderfully freeing and empowering it is to realize that and actually do something about it. As it is, you are both in your own way. Energy is blocked and forward progress is restricted or restrained until you figure this out. Step out of your own way. Try it and see.

Move Forward

It is when you finally have understanding of a person or situation, from their point of view, instead of your own, or from a bigger picture point of view, that you can come to have compassion for them, for yourself, and/or for the situation. From this vantage point – the place of compassion – you can begin to have forgiveness. From forgiveness you have forward progress.

Release

The reason we hang on to experiences, people, events, and the like is because we are still learning something from them. People release when they have learned all they can learn from a certain relationship, pattern, situation, etc. If you are having trouble releasing something, this is why. So, just figure out what you still need to learn. Learn it. And then let it all go.

Release

It is in releasing our patterns that we find true freedom of spirit. Let yourself out of prison. You are the one with the keys.

On Soul Mates

Having a connection with someone does not make him or her your soul mate. It makes it a lesson in Love. Many people from a soul group come together to teach each other things. There is agreement on a soul level to do this work.

On an earth level, some of these lessons may or may not be pleasant; but they are all definitely about Love.

Then when you learn whatever it is you contracted to learn, you both/all move forward on the path. Sometimes you go together and sometimes you do not.

Your soul mate is not the person that makes your life happy, perfect, wonderful, and magical. You have to create your life the way you want it first. The soul mate is the person who shows up after you've already done that and they have done it as well. Everything else is a lesson that you've agreed to learn/teach.

Ask, pray, manifest, not for the soul mate, but for the highest version of your soul that is incarnate at the same time as you.

Power

When we are waiting for something to happen or waiting for someone to call, or similar, we are giving our power away. What this essentially means is that we are not living in the present moment. And the present moment is really all we have. If you do not honor the present moment, you are not honoring yourself and thus, you are giving your power away. So, those of you that are waiting, waiting, waiting. . .stop. Go out and do. Live. Be.

It is not that one should stop dreaming and yearning and looking forward. That's fine. But to live there in your present moment and devote all your energy to what isn't, rather than what is, renders you temporarily powerless.

More on Power

So you want to be rich and famous? So you think you know someone who might help you get there? Ask yourself what are your intentions behind desiring this? Do you perceive rich and famous as having power? Do you think, "If only I had such and such, I would be happy?" There is absolutely zero power in the illusion of having power. Gather your true power inside yourself first. Fill yourself with it. Shine it out, and then see how synchronous your life becomes.

Empty Power

Have you heard of people that win millions of dollars in the lottery and a few years later are completely broke and back where they started? This seems inexplicable to some of us, but it happens. I call this "empty power." There is no power in money in and of itself. There is energy of money.

Money is not power. Essentially, it is neutral. It is we who continue to fuel the illusion of its power. When you realize this, you can effectively free up the flow of its energy to you and it then becomes a non-issue.

These lottery winners that I mentioned most likely had the illusion that money was going to bring them power, happiness, things, whatever. They had perhaps not learned their lessons of real power before this money came to them.

We do not necessarily learn lessons of real power through having money and things. We learn it through remembering who we are and where the real power is. The power is in the love, the ability to love, and the ability to continue to expand that love throughout all adversity, including among other challenges, financial adversity.

The Ego

The ego is what keeps us in our physical bodies. It is also what gets in our way and blocks the healing process. Our egos will lead us down the path of all manner of illusions if we allow it. Try to see through it all. Everything is a lesson in love. Everything. And somewhere in the tiny space between where the ego resides and all of the illusions is the place where miracles occur.

The Ego

I write a lot about the ego – being in it and getting out of it. So, what exactly does it mean when we say, "being in your ego?" The ego essentially is the personality or persona that the soul has taken on for its visit here. In so many ways it is a good thing, although the statement "being in your ego" could be taken to have negative connotations. Most would say to themselves, "I certainly am not in my ego!" We all are to some degree, as that is what keeps us here.

Being "in your ego" does not necessarily mean that you are egotistical. It means that you are in a place where you cannot see the deeper, more connected meaning of events that are transpiring in your life. In a sense, you are "in your own way." You are temporarily blinded by your own disposition. So the challenge is to step aside from that and see the bigger picture; see what lessons you are supposed to learn so that you may learn, grow, and move forward on your path.

Here is a very basic example of "being in your ego:" Someone does not reply to your email and your thinking immediately goes to "The person doesn't like me," "The person isn't responding because they are mad at me," or "I'm not important enough for that person to respond to me," etc. In truth the other person isn't thinking any of those things and perhaps never even got your email.

Now, what are you supposed to learn from that? The things that immediately come to mind are: (1) Why are you giving your power away to this situation? and (2) Why is it all about you? (3) Study your thought pattern here, as thoughts create form.

What Is Going On?

I'm always telling my clients to thank, bless, and release. But in order to do that effectively, one must first totally "get" what is really going on. If someone does something to you that you do not understand, or that hurts you in some manner, one first has to move past the ego's position that they've been wounded or wronged.

This could be a tall order, depending upon your learned and ingrained patterns. If you've made a career out of being a victim, then, it might just be second nature for you to stay in that pattern. In which case you may never see in this lifetime that you have not been wounded, but actually helped in some manner.

To move past the ego, one must look to the bigger picture and try to accept, fully understand, and integrate the truth of it all. We are LOVE. We are teaching each other lessons about love even if it does not appear so. There is and was an agreement on a soul level not to wound you but to help you along your path. Try to see it. It is from that place of truth that you can move forward.

Avoidance

Avoidance is the ego's way of telling itself that it's right. This is the coward's path. I once knew a woman who stopped speaking to her father and never looked back. Something to do with money, as I recall. Her father died last year. She did not attend the funeral.

The same woman stopped speaking to her young grandson one day because of something his mother said or did. This was like a death to the poor child and he spent many years grieving in all sorts of different ways. She cut these people completely out of her life, or so she thinks.

All of these people are still there in spirit, because there is and was an agreement to teach each other life lessons about love. But she apparently cannot see the bigger picture due to the size of her ego, which grows larger with every avoidance.

She will never realize in this lifetime how her actions, or inaction, rippled out and affected many people's lives in a profound manner. Think about this next time you find yourself practicing avoidance. Are you sure you're right or are you simply a coward?

 **Psychic Readings**

We weren't just dropped off here on the planet and left without any way to communicate with Source, guides, and/or angels. So, to some extent every one of us is intuitive and also has some degree of telepathy and/or empathy.

The subject here is about those who purport to be "psychic" and are really just using their intuition, which they have honed to some degree.

The veil has been thinning for quite some time between this world and the other side. And suddenly there arose a crop of people who claim to be able to see.

Some of these people charge ridiculous amounts of money for the pleasure of speaking to them. Be advised that no one knows more about your life than you do. Perhaps you just forgot how to see it and that's okay.

However, make a note that anyone who purports to be a psychic, may or may not be, and is charging some ridiculous amount of money per minute has issues of self-worth and money as it relates to self-worth. Is this the person who is going to help you move forward on your path?

True psychics will charge an equitable amount of money for their time and will tell you things you do not already know. They may tell you things you do not want to hear, but they will help you move forward on the path.

In general, a true psychic will not keep you on a wait list for over three months. Most readings can be scheduled within one month's time if the psychic is truly working as a psychic. Unless they have over 500 people on their wait list, one month to six weeks is a usual time frame.

Do not be duped into thinking that a long wait indicates more than usual access to the truth. It may just indicate a lack of organizational skills. Is this the person who can guide you forward?

Let go of your own illusions about money and time and move forward on your path while you are on someone's wait list. A true psychic will truly make you feel like you are the only client they have.

Person A and Person B

Person A and Person B live in what most would consider a retirement community. On the freeway, quite near the exit ramp, Person B suddenly speeds up and crosses in front of Person A, who is ambling along prudently just under the speed limit. Person B then exits the freeway with this maneuver.

This episode does not cause any physical harm to Person A. However, it stays with her long enough afterward to put some valuable time and energy into writing an indignant letter to her local newspaper. The gist of her letter is that she cannot understand why a retired person would be in such a rush as to cut in front of her like that.

Irrespective of whether or not Person B was wrong in this action, what is it that Person A is not seeing in this situation and why?

More On Person A and Person B

Person A is only seeing things from her limited parameter. Person A is coming from her own perspective. Person A is not seeing that Person B performed this seemingly erratic and unnecessary (from Person A's point of view) maneuver for a reason, other than to startle her, make her angry, or whatever else Person A was feeling.

Person A is making the assumption that, like her, Person B is retired. The truth is

Person B is not retired. Person A is very attached to how Person B made her feel. These are Person A's issues. They do not belong to Person B. As a note, Person B is completely oblivious to how Person A is feeling anyway.

Person B has their own agenda, as well. Person B is a paramedic called suddenly to the scene of an emergency. Unknown to Person A at the time is that one of her friends is involved as a potential victim in the emergency. Person B ends up saving her life.

Things are not always what they seem. It is when we are able to step out of our own ego centered viewpoints that the truth can begin to reveal itself to us.

"When you look into this mirror the reflection's not of you; this window is here to help you see far beyond yourself, it's true." © Dyan Garris 1993-2007. *Voice of the Angels – A Healing Journey Spiritual Cards, The Mirror* card.

The Roar of Intolerance

The growing intolerance we have for each other is getting stronger every day. What is the cause of this, really? In a world where we have "technologied" ourselves to death, it becomes ever more simple to become the great, big shining stars of our own earth-reality drama series.

The clamor for attention is deafening and can even be heard above the incessant, yet seemingly inaudible chatter of constant sound waves, microwaves, radio waves, satellite beams or with whatever else we've bombarded our environment.

At airports, public places, and on the roadways, we act as if our fellow human isn't even human. We act as if we are the only ones that should be allowed in and on such. We act as if our children do not have the right to express their childish and still fragile emotions. Yet we freely express anything we want on our cell phones, and elsewhere, within earshot of anyone. We are, after all, the stars of our show, are we not? So, anyone who is in range gets to know that beyond any doubt.

Have we really become so arrogant, ego centered, egotistical, pompous and power hungry?

What did we do before cell phones? When our plane landed, it landed. We did not call someone immediately upon touchdown to say so. What did we do without caller ID? We simply answered the phone. What did we do without computer and video games? We played board games as a family or a group.

So much of this growing intolerance for our fellow human comes from a completely "I" centered attitude.

There have always been screaming children. There have always been inconveniences on the road and elsewhere. There have always been those who are just plain rude and arrogant and even ignorant. These events and encounters are usually temporary and short-lived, however annoying. And if you look deep enough, there is usually something to be learned from these.

If you have developed patience and tolerance and compassion, these things will stand you in good stead as you travel on the noisy path of life we have created.

Remember, our ancestors simply rode on through all apparent obstacles. Do we have what it takes to do the same? Or have we lost that ability somewhere in the roar?

Ask yourself if it is really so paramount that you and everyone else be able to hear your own voice above the din. There is a great deal to be said for silence and a great deal to be said for the sound of children, screaming or not.

If you quiet the rest of it all down, maybe you can begin to easily hear your own voice again and won't need to shout to be heard. Of course, it is hard to hear much of anything worth listening to while so many are having such deafening and self-indulgent tantrums.

Miracles

Miracles do happen every day if you choose to see it that way. What is a miracle anyway? Is it the answer to your prayers and supplications or is it that wondrous happening that occurs when you aren't focusing on what it is you want?

Often we pray for a miracle and pray and pray and put tremendous energy on the outcome of that prayer. While we are doing that, we are staying attached to the outcome of our prayer. Prayers must go up and out (see "Manifesting and Balloons," page 3) in order for results to return to us.

Why do we remain so attached to outcomes? Do we really believe that by our sheer will and repetitions that we will force a particular outcome? To believe so keeps us in a space of ego and that is not the space from which miracles occur.

Miracles occur in the space where the ego-self completely lets go of what it thinks it wants and allows the universe to bring forth its glory in ways that you cannot possibly imagine.

If you insist on keeping a limited parameter, this is what will return to you, limits. Open to infinite possibilities and this is what will return to you, miracles.

Timing

Yesterday as I was driving, a very strange thing happened. A man jumped out of his car and started running. A nearby policeman jumped out of his car and started running after the man. The timing on this was such that if I had been in that exact spot one split second later I would have hit the man with my car and/or hit the policeman. There is a possibility that I could have been involved in a shooting as well. This entire episode, if it had unfolded in a different way, could have affected my life in a multitude of ways.

The fact is whatever it was that was going on was not my karma, had nothing to do with me, was not supposed to alter my course; and therefore events unfolded quite differently. I was allowed smooth sailing on my path. The universe knows its timing and we must trust in that. Everything happens (or doesn't happen) for a reason. Trust that.

The Sweetness of Life

Here is a piece of cake. Your mind tells you it's sweet. But you don't really know until you actually taste it, do you? So, are you afraid of the cake? Are you afraid of tasting it? It's just a piece of cake.

Do you remember the movie, *Michael*? It starred John Travolta as the angel Michael. Do you remember that he danced and battled and enjoyed and lived his brief time here to the fullest?

That is because he remembered what a gift it was to be in the physical body.

He had a mission. He knew the truth of how things were to unfold and weave together, even when the others doubted. He just knew. So he fulfilled his mission while orchestrating, encouraging, and prompting the others to move forward on their path even if it made no sense to them at the time.

And perhaps it is only from the other side of life that we remember how special it is to be incarnated here in the physical. We are to experience it all, love, laughter, pain, joy, sorrow, and most importantly, sweetness.

Take your sweet moments where you find them, whether it be cake, the thought of cake, a shared laugh, a birth, a special kiss, a very intimate moment remembered, loving and kind words, the look in someone's eyes, a good and fine gourmet meal, or even a shared bologna sandwich.

These little moments of joy are what make up the fabric of your tapestry in this lifetime. They may seem few and far between; so take them all in and remember them with every fiber of your being forever. This is what is known as and ends up as cellular memory.

We do remember the joy and love that we experience, and we remember it on every level. It's what you take out of here – it's the very last thing you think about and express – and it's what you bring with you next time. Why wait until the end?

And hopefully, the joy overshadows the pain. There is no reason to lose the sweetness of life. You can always carry it in your mind, just like this picture of cake. Enjoy your cake and consider eating it too.

The Measure of Success

We are taught from a very young age to measure everything. Someone handed us an invisible yardstick and we've carried it around for years measuring and measuring. We measure our height and weight and waistlines. We measure our growth and our progress with someone else's idea of milestones. We measure our food and our food ingredients because we are afraid to use our intuition. Some are even afraid of nourishment.

We measure our IQs. We measure our bank accounts. We measure ourselves against others. For years the size of one's car was an accepted measure of one's supposed success.

Lately, we use the quantity of the things that we have as a measure of success. We must be ok if we have three cars in the garage, two or three houses, a 401(k), stock options, and whatever else passes as someone's illusion of how success is supposed to show up.

Just exactly when did we become pieces of paper, inches, centimeters, teaspoons, and 1/4 cups?

When we expect and desire "success" to return to us as pieces of paper, this is what we are manifesting; and eventually, if we put enough energy on it, it will return to us that way.

Pieces of paper in and of themselves are completely worthless. It is the energy we put behind them that gives them the power they have today. It is an illusion. It is the under-"lying" belief systems that shape perception.

Money is simply energy. Our fair exchange of energy could just as easily be beads, corn, guns or butter. It doesn't matter. It is energy and thoughts about such things that fuel the power of matter.

If we insist upon "success" showing up and returning to us as money or things, we then limit the universe's ability to bring us what we need in other ways. We limit ourselves to our version of the story. In our attempts to be so big, have we really become so small?

The true measure of a man is not found in his wallet but in his heart. The only thing that is real is love. It's what everyone goes out of here saying, thinking about, and remembering. Everything else is an illusion. So, how successful are you?

Nail Soup

When I was a child, someone gave me a book, *Nail Soup*. Essentially, it was about someone making something really tasty out of nothing. I believe we should take all the ingredients in our refrigerator and make something excellent out of them. Make the most of what you have. In the meantime, here is a little soup for you.

What is Real?

Like a comfy pair of old shoes, we put
on our learned patterns. Patterns of
co-dependence, abuse, and self abuse
were learned from our "tribe." This is not
who we are. The part we often do not
realize is that our tribe is not necessarily
our soul group. We did not come here to
imitate the patterns of our tribe. Among
other things, we came to be the best
we can be and do our soul work that we
chose when we were together in spirit
with our collective souls. It is time to shed
the base lessons that we have learned
here and focus on our real purpose.

Remember though, to honor the lessons
of the "tribe." They are the ones who
agreed to act as hosts to us and give us
a platform for our lessons in love and our
lessons of the soul.

Without these illusions we cannot get to
what is real. Thank, honor, and forgive.
Now, get new shoes and move forward!

Travel On

We are all just travelers on the path. Everyone you meet here is a fellow traveler. Some deliver messages. Some stay for a while. Some pass on. Some stay with you for the rest of your time here and some just pass through. Every encounter, every nuance, and every word has meaning.

It is what you do with it all that matters. It is like taking what you learned in school – what you were just taking notes on at the time – and applying it now in a real world sense to your journey. And make sure now to honor the journey of the fellow traveler.

"As you travel on this journey, with seven angels too, remember that we are as one voice – Mother-Father-God-and-You." © Dyan Garris 1993-2007. *From Voice of the Angels – A Healing Journey Spiritual Cards, The Mother* card.

No Regrets

When you find yourself at odds with someone, it is not a good feeling. What you are feeling is disharmony between mind, body, and spirit. The choices to correct this are simple. You can choose to stay in the disharmony or not stay in it. It is simple to correct this imbalance if you can get out of your ego, get out of your point of view and return to the only thing that is real. That is Love.

Forgive the person and move ahead on the path. Let it go. Get out of your own way and move forward instead of staying stuck in something so unhealthy to every part of your being. Are you mad at someone for something they are not equipped to give you? Life is short. Don't take any moment of it for granted. We do not know when we will be called home and we should return home with absolutely no regrets.

No Regrets

We do not know the number of our days, hours, time here. Live your life with no regrets. If you've done things you aren't proud of, start getting them in perspective. Make amends to whomever, if necessary, and to yourself. We cannot change the past but we can change our view of it.

Look upon everything you have chosen to do as a learning experience. Now take all that learning and do something constructive with it. Extricate yourself from the bindings you have tied around yourself. You are only a victim if you allow yourself to be.

Be clear on what your issue is and what is not your issue. Free yourself and move forward in gratitude for the gifts you have been given: breath, life, free will, and most of all, the capacity to love. Love endures everlasting.

No Regrets

After a holiday season of comparing ourselves to our relatives and friends, do you feel a little less than par? We are living in a world that is struggling to ground itself; and in the process, there is much focus on the root chakra issues and pleasures. We must remember who we are in that paradox. Who are we without our money and earthly possessions? Must we lose it all to bring us to remembrance? This isn't necessary unless you make it so.

Get out of your fear-based attitudes and belief systems. You can do anything you set your minds to. Stop comparing yourselves with others, no matter who they are. Stop trying to come up to everyone else's expectations. Be who you are.

Be not sad. Be not afraid. Fill your soul with laughter and music. These help shift the vibrations, not only of your personal realm, but on a global level as well. When we are vibrationally attuned, it is easier to make major shifts in consciousness.

How Hard Can It Be?

So much of life here is perspective and perception. We've all heard the clichés, "the glass is half full," or "the glass is half empty." Try a new perception: "How hard can it be?" Things are only truly daunting, confusing, or intimidating if we perceive them to be so. Let go of the need to control. Let go of the fear of the loss of control. These are the underpinnings and foundations of the root of all things apparently insurmountable.

You can do anything you put your mind to. You can do anything that you can imagine. Remember that you do not have to do it all at once. Take steps toward your goals; plant seeds all along the way. And don't fret about the "how." Soon you will look up and you will find that you have reached those goals.

For example, do not say, "I must lose 50 pounds in three months." This may seem overwhelming. Instead, simply release the need for the weight and the rest will follow. Release your preconceived ideas about how things occur. Open to love. Open to miracles. How hard can it be? Only as hard as you make it.

Center

Somewhere in the silence and empty space between the in-breath and the out-breath is where you find yourself. It is where you get centered. If we are not paying attention to our breathing this way via meditation or breath work, it can be challenging to find one's spirit and the focus becomes the ego instead. Take a few minutes to get centered in your "self" every day. Unexpected or unsettling events are best dealt with from a position of self-empowerment rather than from ego.

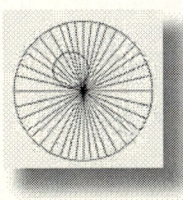

Star Light

Your life should not be a stage for playing out your unresolved dramas or traumas with people who were not responsible for creating the drama or trauma in the first place. It is not helpful to misplace anger onto someone else. This is a pattern of abuse.

Look to your own responsibility in the creation of your circumstances. To do otherwise renders you a victim and allows the abuse patterns to continue on and on. You choose where you are, where you want to be and where you have been. You can truly blame no one else. So stand in your light and in your power and be respectful of one another even if you are strangers. If you can see through the illusion, you will realize that we aren't strangers to one another at all. Extend yourself in one small way, even if you feel over extended. Everything will come back to you eventually.

Fire Pit

It is important to be completely aware of what your issue is and what is not your issue. Let other people think whatever they want. Your only issue should be how you act or react to whatever it is they are doing or saying or have done or said. To become upset at the actions of another is to give your power away to that person or situation. You then feed it and give fuel to the fire. Take back your power.

Why walk through another person's fire pit while dancing to their tune?

This is as if you are hired entertainment, but there is no reward for you at the end of the performance. You have your own fire to tend to and your own individual beat, do you not? A much richer reward awaits on the other side of walking through your own hot coals.

The Box

The vibrations to the planet are increasingly violent and destructive. Certainly violence and destruction have been in the world for as long as one can remember. And so many of us have become desensitized to it as we become increasingly wrapped up in our individual dramas and reveries, wants, needs, and desires. However, these influences are increasing now and we must do something about it or we are headed nowhere. What can you do, you ask? It is very simple.

We must develop tolerance and compassion for each other and learn to take a step out of ego. Being wrapped up in our ego perceptions keeps our spirits confined. And that is not just tolerance and compassion when convenient. It is every day. We can begin to do this on a small scale from our own diminutive platforms.

For example, if someone cuts in front of you in a line, or cuts you off in your car, or does or says something equally rude or insensitive, you have a choice in that moment as to how you will react or act. From the ego's point of view, it seems natural or justified to be equally or more rude.

Here is a suggestion for a behavior change: Simply do not respond or react in a negative or defensive way, even if you have always done so before. This is not to suggest that one become a doormat. Kindness begets kindness. Tolerance begets tolerance. And compassion begets the same. We must start somewhere. Loving vibrations have so much power and they do have the power to change the world with their ripple effect. Believe it.

So today do one small thing differently than you would normally do. Show love, compassion, kindness and tolerance in everyday situations where you normally would not. Let's take a step out of the ego container before we all find ourselves in a different kind of box.

The Song

Your life is like a song. A song is made up of musical notes. You can stay in any one octave or chord or keep on playing one individual note, or you can move around in any sequence or direction you choose. But the point is that you make up the melody of your life. You decide if it's a symphony or not. You decide if it's safer or more melodic for you to stay within one area of your instrument or move around, up, down, play in duet, or whatever.

On any instrument, extremes, middle ground, and infinite combinations can be reached or composed. Decide whether you will make noise, harmony, or a brand new song. Within this particular paradigm everyone has the capacity to be Mozart.

Free Will

Free will is one of the greatest gifts that has been bestowed upon us. While it's true that one single moment and one single choice can change our lives, it is important to remember there are no wrong decisions. Whatever you choose and whatever path you find yourself on, you will learn the same lesson you are supposed to learn.

Everything does ultimately weave together for the highest good. If you find yourself doing things you don't want to do, realize that your free will choices brought you there and you have the power to change anything you desire. You are not a victim of circumstances beyond your control unless you believe that you are.

The Messy Room

Cleaning an extremely messy room can appear to be a daunting task if one steps in and looks at the chaos as a whole. Focus on one specific corner or one area of the room and clean that up first. While doing that, do not look at the whole. Do not allow yourself to become overwhelmed by the big picture. Continue cleaning up one small area at a time. Put all of your focus on that particular area. Leave the room temporarily if you must. Enlist the help of others if you need.

When you return, focus on what you have accomplished, rather than on what still needs to be done. The room did not get in this condition overnight. Realize that it may take some time and effort to get it in order. By cleaning and focusing on small areas, your entire room will soon be clear and ready for whatever new things will come your way. Nothing new can come in if there is no room.

Fair Exchange of Energy

We go to our jobs. We do our work. We get a paycheck and maybe benefits in return. Some would say this is a fair exchange of energy. Money is, after all, simply energy. However, a fair exchange of energy does not necessarily have to do with money and is not necessarily limited to our earthly conception of this concept of our earthly expectations. Whatever you need returns to you in some way. So, extend yourself to others, put your light out there, and know that you receive whatever you give.

"Through love and light your answers dear will truly be here soon; this illumination will shine clearly then even by night's moon." © Dyan Garris 1993-2007. *Voice of the Angels – A Healing Journey Spiritual Cards, The Light* card.

Transformation

There are many deaths in life. Deaths of friends, loved ones, and relationships are just a few. Death is simply transformation and it's something we encounter and practice many, many times along the path.

Transformation is not to be feared, but embraced, rather. Where there is an apparent ending, truly exists opportunity for new beginning. Thus is the cycle of life. Let your loved ones, friends, and relationships go gracefully and peacefully so that life can begin anew.

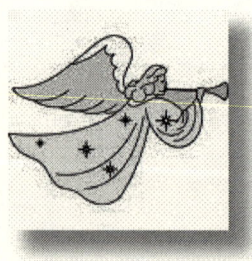

Open To Love

Wherever we have fear, we have the absence of Love. Wherever we do not have Love, we block ourselves from forward progress. We remain then, in ego; and being in ego brings only more vibration of ego into our lives. We attract that which we vibrate and resonate to. We attract that which we believe in. Fear begets more fear. Being in loving space allows channels to open, easily and effortlessly. Inhale and exhale beautiful, pure, white, loving light. Why question your worthiness? You are worthy. Why allow someone or something to define your value? You are valuable. Vibrate and be open to the frequency of Love and watch miracles occur.

 **So and So**

So many of us derive our self-esteem from the outside. One of the challenges is to begin to define who we really are from the inside. Many ask, "When will so and so call me?" or "What is wrong with me that so and so doesn't have feelings for me?" Has it occurred to you that nothing is wrong with you and perhaps it is "so and so" that has the real problem? Start with that. Don't be so willing to give all your power away to the perhaps misguided opinion of "so and so." Reach inside and figure out who you really are without the illusions of power, such as money; and particularly figure out who you are without "so and so." And so it is.

Are You Fortunate?

Can you see the starry sky, the ocean, the mountains, your child's face? Can you still look at icicles and snowflakes with wonder? Can you hear music, words, laughter? Can you feel pain, sorrow, optimism, joy, happiness, and love? Can you taste all the wonders the world has to offer? Yes, you are fortunate. Live this day with your whole self no matter how it shows up. Feel your feelings, whatever they are. You are alive!

Poverty Consciousness

Poverty consciousness is a belief system that we create within ourselves. It originates from the fear of the lack of something, and in this case that something is money. We create whatever it is we believe. There is no power in fear. The power is in the Love.

Limitations

Whatever your core belief system, that is what you create and live. If you believe there are limitations, then there are limitations. Really study your thought patterns and figure out what you are creating. You can truly do anything you put your mind, body, heart and soul into. There is always a way to accomplish whatever you desire to accomplish. Limitations exist only if you believe they do. Challenge yourself to move beyond what you think you see or what you think is there for you. Why limit yourself? What are you afraid of? Open your mind to infinite possibilities.

Pixie Dust

A garden does not sprout up overnight and some things in the garden take longer than others. If you want a full garden, you have to plant, cultivate, water, and tend. But no amount of fussing will make things grow faster than in their own time. Have patience. Things will change. In the meantime, a little pixie dust is always a good thing! Let your mind go to the possibility of magic and miracles.

The Principle of Mother

At times we are all called upon to exhibit the principle of mother. This should not include enabling, but rather, empowering. The challenge is to teach rather than do it all for a person. Through this process one must keep their patience, understanding, and acceptance of the cyclical nature of the universe. All things ripen in their time and this cannot be rushed. While waiting for this process to unfold, think and vibrate to unconditional love. This requires one to move away from one's ego position and attachment to outcome, no matter how difficult that seems. Remember, teach them to do it for themselves rather than do it for them. This ultimately lifts us ALL up and the result is multi-dimensional, rather than linear.

Re

We are all being called upon to live more multi-dimensionally. Try to see the bigger picture. We must remember who we are. We must remember our connection to each other. We must remember the love we came in with. The power is in the love, not in the fear. Change and transformation may seem daunting, but only if we believe them to be so. We create whatever we believe.

Don't rip your whole house up in a *re*decorating frenzy. Start with one room at a time. Do not concern yourself with the judgments of others. *Re*decorate in any way that pleases you. Take your time and enjoy the process. Listen to your inner voice. Attend to the balance of the physical body. Stay away from extremes. Balance is a keyword. Take time to *re*group, *re*organize, or *re*think. Have faith.

Lessons In Love

We are being challenged to see the bigger picture and to see beyond what we think we see. We are being challenged to see beyond our money or our lifestyles and our previous definitions of ourselves. We are being challenged to move off of our ego positions. Everyone presently in your life and everyone in your past has been there or is there for a reason. No matter what it looks like, it all truly is a lesson in Love. Everyone and everything has led you to where you are and, if you are willing to see it, will lead you to your life's purpose. Thank them all, bless them, and release them so you can move forward on your path.

Relating

In any communication with another, do not assume that they are coming from your point of view. You can safely assume that they are not. Everyone has their own set of experiences and perceptions that they base their reality on. You have yours. They have theirs. You can best relate by just saying your truth and letting them say theirs. Meet somewhere in the middle.

Breathe

Spend less time being outraged and more time focusing on our true connection. Mother Teresa had it right when she said we have forgotten that we all belong to each other. Breathe!

Open

You are where you are because of choices you have made. Accept or even celebrate those choices. It does no good to rue them. Take a fresh approach to an old way of doing things or an old way of relating. Do one thing for someone else completely from your heart today and without thought of return. Do one thing differently today. This opens the mind and subsequently the spirit and shifts the vibration of the entire universe by its ripple effect. And if you listen closely then, in a moment of silent gratitude, you may even hear angels singing. May Grace bless your day.

Entitlement

What happened to honor, integrity and respect? Why are we entitled to be nurtured or enabled? Why do we feel entitled to anything? This is the ego in our way. The truth is that the only one entitled to anything is the helpless infant. It is time to grow up and take responsibility for whatever we've created. Learn to honor and respect everyone and every single thing and person in your life. Remember to thank them for being a part of your life. This sets the stage for honor and respect to flow into your life.

Entitlement

When we feel we are owed something, we are being in our ego. We are being self-absorbed. The truth is no one owes you anything. We come in with nothing. We leave with nothing, and we are responsible for creating everything in-between.

If you feel that you were the victim of a bad childhood or a bad relationship, that is where you stay. You render yourself a victim. If you continue to feel that someone owes you something for that childhood or that relationship, you are creating and perpetuating karmic bonds.

You will continue to attract similar situations and energies until you can forgive. In forgiveness you release yourself from the bonds that keep you in the same patterns.

Do not keep insisting that the entities that you feel have hurt you or slighted you be the ones to do the forgiving. To insist so is to give your power away. In forgiveness you release yourself from the need for entitlement. Do this and be completely free.

 **Change What You Can**

Face the truth, whatever it is. We must face the consequences of our past decisions. Make an alternate plan and do not repeat the same actions. Forgiveness is key to moving forward. Balance is needed. Do your best to balance the physical, mental, and spiritual. It does no good to get angry. That is a waste of energy and does not change anything. Accept the things you cannot change and devote all your energy to changing the things that you can change.

Intentions

Study your intentions. Are they pure of heart or do you desire something for yourself? Intentions that are pure circulate love back to us. Intentions that are ego driven bring back ego laden situations and resistance. Manipulation gets you nowhere. If you don't get out of this ego driven mode, you stay stuck and the old patterns continue to repeat.

Intentions

In analyzing any situation, always look to a person's intentions and look to your own intentions. If you are attached to outcomes or trying to manipulate a situation for personal gain, this keeps you stuck in your lower chakras. If you approach any situation with pure of heart and loving intentions, then that situation will always be lifted up no matter how it appears on the earth plane.

Letting Go

It is so easy to say, "Just let go." But it really is a process. The first step in letting anything go is to simply accept what IS. Usually you cannot change or control "what IS." This does not mean that you give up. This means that you simply accept the facts of something you cannot change. You must accept it.

Once you get firmly in that space, the energy shifts, allowing new pathways to open. If you stay in a space of trying to control or change something that is completely unchangeable, such as physical death or death of a relationship, you are then blocking yourself and wasting the energy of your spirit. You are in your own way on the path.

There are some things you can change (yourself) and some things you cannot change (anyone else). One must know and fully accept the difference in order to move forward.

So, today practice the process of letting go. And then allow dreams and visions of the future to flow to you. Be at peace in your spirit and the rest follows.

Let Go

Life is a series of choices. You have chosen with whom you will do your lessons. Everyone that shows up in your life shows up because you have an agreement with him or her to do so. If you were wrong about something in the past, step up and say so. There is no point in holding ill will for decades or even lifetimes. These things grate on your soul and it does no good to carry them around. Ultimately they become very heavy luggage for us all. Let go.

Judgments

Everyone in your life is some kind of reflection of you, even if you don't realize it. When you make judgments on people, you should look to yourself first. For example, if you make the statement that someone is being petty, you should then look to yourself and see where you are being petty. One of the ways you are being petty is by saying someone else is petty. Judgment bounces back upon us. Everything is a reflection. Think twice before pronouncing judgment.

More On Judgments

How many times have you looked at someone and made a judgment about who they are or what they are about? How many times have you looked at a book or CD cover and made a judgment about what is inside? How many times have you driven by a house and made a judgment about what the inside is like? And do you know how many times you missed out on something valuable because of those judgments?

Open your minds to the possibility that things are not always what they seem. Do not be blinded to the truth by the bright light of your own ego-self.

Meditation

Meditation really is just connection. We have forgotten how to just "be." It isn't difficult or mysterious. It is a mindful focus. Quiet the chatter of the conscious mind and follow the breath as it moves through your physical body. If one can quiet down the chatter, one can shift one's focus from all the earthly tasks, begin to connect with something higher, and get in touch with one's spirit again.

It all starts with breathing. Just let go of everything else for ten minutes. Feel yourself grounded and centered in yourself. You don't have to "do" anything. You don't have to have any expectations. Just breathe and relax and see how much better you feel. You will perhaps then find yourself more able to deal with earthly challenges as you connect to the very truth of yourself.

Manifesting

It is when we are stuck in our "self" mode that we cannot manifest. This mode is immobilizing and fills us with fear. Fear blocks love. Love is the seat of creation. If you can move yourself out of "self" mode and recenter yourself into your true center, you can move into manifesting mode. You can create. Get over your "self." Literally.

Manifesting

Start the day by being grateful for what you have, rather than focusing on what you don't have. Realize that you are where you are by your choices. Take responsibility for them. This keeps you from being a victim. Victims are powerless and you are not powerless.

You have free will and you always have a choice even if you might not like the choice. You have the power to create your life any way you want, even if you do not think so.

Start by visualizing your desires. Put a lot of loving, positive energy on it and then let it go up and out into the heavenly realms. Then go about your day as if you have already received. Love is the most powerful thing in the universe. Let it flow to you and from you.

More On Manifesting

You have the power to change your life. We create with our thoughts. It becomes a matter of what you focus on. Study your thought patterns. Garbage in, garbage out. It's just like a computer. You are the programmer. Decide what you want to create and put all your focus there.

When you find yourself thinking about things in the old way or a negative way, focus on changing those thoughts to the positive; or focus on a new way. Do not let fear creep in. Fear blocks love. Live as if you have already received. See, feel, breathe, live, and know beyond any doubt that you have already received. This opens pathways for your desires to manifest.

Reflection On Manifesting

Sometimes we think we are manifesting, but what we are really doing is demanding that the universe immediately provide us with what we desire and in the time frame we direct. This is not manifesting. It is a tantrum. This demanding, controlling and dictating blocks and negates our manifesting process.

A key part of manifesting is to let go and trust. If you had an object you wanted fixed, would you take it somewhere to be fixed and then proceed to tell the person how to fix it? This is counter-productive. If you knew how to fix it yourself, you would.

So then trust that the universe hears, sees, and knows your needs, wants and desires and is knitting and weaving together the correct and most beautiful garment that fits you perfectly. Trust.

The Heart

Why are we so willing to open our root chakras to others and not our hearts? This is backward. First open your hearts. The rest follows. Love resides in the heart, not the root. The root is the place to express the love of the heart, not the other way around. We cannot "get" love this way. To try to express love only in the root chakra while keeping the heart closed keeps us locked in the base patterns of the root chakra. Open your hearts.

Celebrate

It is important to embrace who we are. Today find one quality about yourself that you really love. Wrap it around yourself like a warm, soft blanket and completely embrace yourself. You are here for a reason, but you don't have to fret about why. Just let things unfold, like an excellent novel. Celebrate the day. Be joyful.

Blanket Of Love

So you wake up and you feel empty. Maybe you have everything you ever dreamed of and you still feel empty. Maybe you had dreams and aspirations for yourself and you find you have not lived up to them. It doesn't matter. What matters is the emptiness.

The wholeness that you seek does not come from outside things. It does not come from another person or people. It does not come from sex or money or children or a 401(k) or cars or houses or anything else we deem valuable on this earth plane.

The wholeness comes from getting in touch with your spirit. It comes from seeing through the illusions of this lifetime. Yes, we need these things – or so we think – but these things should not define our entire existence or dictate the mood of our time here.

We spend so much time living life in our root chakras that our hearts are not open.

To truly be one with the universe is to have every chakra open, front and back, and each connected to the other – connect the dots! And to truly be connected is to feel ourselves in every chakra, not just the perceived safety of the root.

Get out of the illusion of outside things or people being able to make you happy. Make yourself happy first in your spirit. Be grateful for every day and every single event of every day and the simple beauty of the day. Then the energy that you seek will flow to you. Remember, you co-create every moment of your life.

So take responsibility for your life – every moment of it. See where you are not Love. See things as the lesson in Love that they are. Learn the lessons and move on. Graduate.

Do not make anyone else responsible for your happiness or lack of it. You have the power to create such. If you view yourself as powerless, then you are so. Take into your spirit the beauty that surrounds you and remember to honor all the things you usually take for granted. These are the threads of the fabric of your life.

We have so much abundance and we fail to perceive it. Today try to see what you do have. Try to get in touch with your spirit and not just your illusions. And when you put the blanket of life around you, actually think about the construction of it. These are the threads of your life.

Ego Trips

The ego will lead us on many a wild journey. That's why it's called an ego trip. It is when we figure out what is real and what is an illusion that we make spiritual progress. It is challenging to get out of the ego because sometimes the perceptions of the ego are so deeply ingrained that they feel real. We get stuck in our perceptions and our point of view. Most people believe what they think they see. Most people cannot see beyond that because of the illusions they were taught. Today see if you can figure out where your ego leads you astray. Keep in mind there is only one true thing in the universe and that is Love. Everything else is an illusion.

See The Bigger Picture

It is time to look beyond yourself and see the bigger picture. Progress can be made if you do not spend time daydreaming or focusing on yourself. Others may need your assistance. Put your oxygen mask on first before assisting others. If you don't, you will be of no service to anyone else because you won't be able to breathe. Let go of previous patterns.

Do not be blinded by the light of your own image. It is time to transform the lower into the higher. Try to get out of your root chakra patterns and raise your energy enough to live life in your upper chakras as well.

Saving

The truth is no one can "save" you. You must first save yourself. To expect someone to save you is to put yourself in the victim role, thus giving your power away to the saver. First put your oxygen mask on the places in your life that need to breathe. Become full of life again. Gather all your power back. Call your spirit back to you. Then you will find that you do not need "saving." You are then no longer a victim, but a whole, living, breathing, loving, person with much to contribute. Open your heart.

Healing Opportunities

It won't do you any good to keep your feelings buried, repressed or hidden. What is hidden will bubble up to the surface. The purpose is so that you can transmute, heal, grow, and transform. The energy may feel quite intense, but the old ways of dealing with such are truly at an end.

It is time to face the energy squarely in the face. Feel your feelings, whatever they are. If you continually stuff your feelings down, they get stuck in the body, eventually causing physical distress. Keep your focus on "up and out." Be aware. Be ready.

When the emotions boil out of the pot, instead of reverting to old patterns, recognize these moments as the opportunities for healing that they are, rather than focusing on the mess that is made when something boils out of the pot.

Greatness

Everyone in your life is a great gift to you and you to them. You are teaching each other lessons in Love. Today, honor someone in your life, even if it is in a small way. The purpose of your life may be made up of a series of the small things you do.

Not everything has to show up in some grand way. And keep in mind that these "grand" forums are something that we humans have created as a way to showcase that which we perceive as "great."

Greatness doesn't necessarily require a huge audience. So go about your day and know that you can achieve greatness simply through Love. Do you really need thunderous applause to validate your earthly parking ticket? You can validate it yourself if you choose.

Through The Fog

Lighten up a little today and try to regain your sense of humor. Life has been challenging in a variety of areas. The key is to figure out what the real lessons are behind the illusions of money, relationship challenges, etc. See if you can find the theme or pattern. Then you can take steps toward change. So, even if you can't see clearly now, laugh a little. It's good medicine and its sound will travel through the fog like a shining beacon.

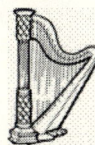

The Heart Of The Matter

Now more than ever we must lift each other up, rather than tear each other down. This kind of behavior keeps us stuck in our root chakras rather than raising our energy to higher levels of consciousness. The energy of sex and money resides in the root chakra; and if we're stuck there entrenched in those issues, it doesn't leave a lot of room for love. We love truly with our hearts, not our base. Try to live from your heart today. Don't let anyone or anything drag you down.

"Open your heart now to the light and let it shine from deep inside; a transformation can occur if you are willing not to hide." © Dyan Garris 1993-2007. *Voice of the Angels – A Healing Journey Spiritual Cards, The Heart* card.

The 101st Time

Sometimes life presents us with challenges that seem confusing and insurmountable. Sometimes you can read something a hundred times and it makes no sense. But on the 101st time, suddenly everything becomes crystal clear; you can see your way out and you know what to do. Never give up. If something makes no sense, keep trying until you've exhausted all possibilities. It isn't over until it is over.

And remember, when one door closes, another opens. There is always a new beginning after an ending and there is a reason for everything. Trust in the higher powers. So hang in there; keep trying and look forward to illuminations and fresh starts.

Moving Out Of Ego Perceptions

Our ego perceptions are what keep us locked in our various patterns. We become stuck in those perceptions. To move out of that position in any interaction, try simply to see things from someone else's vantage point. When you do that, it moves you out of your own way, even if only for a few moments. Just doing this opens a doorway for healing to begin. Try it.

Perceptions

Our perceptions become our reality. One should contemplate just where these perceptions came from in the first place. One should contemplate just what they have their minds, bodies and spirits invested in and decide if they still want to own these perceptions.

You have the power to change your life if you do not persist in giving your power away. Contemplate the true meaning of this. You have the power to change the way you perceive anything, the way you react or not react, thus changing your patterns, thus changing your perceptions, and consequently, your reality. Walk through all of the illusions that you have created for yourself. Call your spirit back to you and be free.

Self-Love

If we expect others to love and honor us, we must first love and honor ourselves. If we are engaging in self-destructive or self-defeating thought patterns or behaviors, we must first eliminate them. Study where these patterns came from in the first place. They came from the outside. They came from someone else's belief systems. Make time for yourself and honor yourself even if it is only in one small way. This begins to open a pathway for the energies we truly desire to come in.

Your Spiritual House

Clean your spiritual house like you clean the physical house you live in. Get rid of the things that no longer make sense. Get rid of things or people or experiences that no longer fit. However, don't just throw them mindlessly away in the garbage. Thank them, honor them, bless them and forgive them, if necessary; and then gently release them. In this way you open the pathway for new people and experiences to come into your life. You open the portal to growth and transformation. To not do this is to continually repeat your patterns. This blocks growth and gets you nowhere. Get out of your own way and allow things to flow. Clean up.

Money Flow

To allow money to flow, we must first figure out where the flow is stuck. Start looking at money as energy instead of allowing pieces of paper to define who you are. Then you will begin to be able to unblock the flow. Look at exactly what belief systems were taught to you regarding money. This is key.

When did you start equating your value as a person with pieces of paper? This was taught to you. You did not come in with this belief system.

Money/Self-Worth

Your core belief systems about money were taught to you. That means these are someone else's belief systems. You have the power and ability to change the patterns you carry around with you regarding money and how it relates to your self-worth. We carry these patterns in our root chakra. Equating money (pieces of paper) with our self-worth is an illusion. Limitations are an illusion. Contemplate.

Acceptance

Accept your mission in this lifetime, however that shows up. Accept it completely and with all of your being. Honor yourself and this incarnation. You are where you are because of your choices. Everyone and everything is a reflection. There are reasons for all. Allow others to exercise their free will. Accept that there are those things that you cannot change and know that you cannot change them for a very good reason, even it seems otherwise. Do not impose your will upon others. Allow, flow, relax, and just be.

While you are waiting for the energy to shift into forward gear, do what you can do. Plant your seeds. Don't rip up your entire garden just because you can't see anything sprouting up. It's there. It's just below the surface right now. Make your plans. Let go of the past.

Sometimes, in any given situation, all you can do is wait. One must respect the law of free will. While you are waiting, remember that you have free will too. You can choose to force the issue or just wait it out. One of the lessons here is patience.

It is very loving to just let someone figure things out while you step aside from your ego and let things unfold. Tread lightly and let the higher powers weave things together first. This may take some time on the earth plane.

Let go. Trust. And go with the flow. Wait confidently and know that all is knitting together for the highest good, no matter how it looks at the moment.

Moving Forward

What is hidden can be revealed. Apply new ways of thinking to old situations instead of using the same thought patterns that you've always used. There is more to be uncovered and revealed if you just allow things to flow to you without judgment. Don't stay stuck in repetitive cycles. You can make progress in relationships by remaining calm, listening and fully taking in what is being communicated.

Study where you have been deluding yourself. Face your fears and thus eliminate them. Take off the rose colored glasses and see the truth. Make adjustments, shifts, and changes where needed. Get out of your own way and move forward on the path.

Remember

We are all connected threads intertwined and woven into the same cloth. Does it take tragedy and drama for us to remember this?

Validation

Why do we seek approval and validation from the outside? Validation and approval seeking are patterns we learned in childhood. As adults we continue to seek approval mainly because we have always done it and we still view it as a way to receive love. Patterns perpetuate.

The problem with needing outside validation is that one then needs it constantly. If one doesn't receive it continually, one doesn't know who they are. One doesn't feel grounded. One wonders what's wrong with them.

In this situation the mind, body and spirit are not balanced. And thus a great deal of energy is expended on this pattern and the energy becomes self-directed and self-focused, rather than focused on shining one's spirit light outward.

Validation should and can come from the inside. Patterns can be broken and replaced. One only needs to become aware of a pattern and then it is their choice whether or not to release it.

Anxiety and Fear

Anxiety and fear come from the fear of the loss of control. In order to conquer such, first accept the things you cannot change. You can change yourself and you can change your reactions and your behaviors. That's it. You cannot change anyone else in any way; so just accept that. Don't spend one precious iota of life force energy worrying or being anxious about any situation or person that you cannot change. To do so is wasting the gift of life. What is is what is.

Next, simply do your best at all times. Give whatever you are engaged in, in any given moment, 100% of your attention and effort. Be not afraid or intimidated by anyone or anything. Just do the best you can do and do it with your whole self. To do otherwise is to put yourself in a victim position.

Remember as well, that form follows thought; so if you are focusing a lot of energy on being fearful and afraid about something, you tend to draw the thing you fear right to you. Why not shift your focus and energy to the energy of success instead. It's a much more powerful energy.

Third, do not give your power away. Gather the power of your wonderful spirit inside yourself and project it out to the world like a beacon of light. Do not let anyone make you nervous, anxious, or fearful. If you feel that way, you are giving your power over to that person or that situation. And that is something you can change. Have a worry free day.

Go With The Flow

Imagine you are floating in a raft, like the raft shown below. The raft has no oars. You cannot steer it. You cannot make it go any faster. You are simply floating in your raft. The clear inscription on the raft is "Trust." You can choose to make it a pleasant journey and use the time wisely, perhaps for contemplation, regrouping, or re-generation. Many people find floating in the raft with no control to be very frustrating. Just continue to plant your seeds. Eventually they will grow and you will reap what you have sown.

"A raft is here for traveling on to places yet unknown; surrender now to love and light and see how much you've grown." © Dyan Garris 1993-2007. *Voice of the Angels – A Healing Journey Spiritual Cards, The Raft* card.

Something Special

We all have something special to do. Don't doubt that. It may not seem so at times, but it's true. Move along the path and honor yourself and every person you encounter. Be grateful for the day. Be grateful for all of the lessons. They are all about Love, even if they don't seem so. Focusing on this will help you stay grounded and centered in the face of whatever comes your way.

Try to do everything from a place of loving intention. Everything eventually weaves together for the highest good. If you are having a difficult time, know that you are not alone and that there are reasons for it. They will eventually become clear. Learn, grow, and awaken.

Life's Purpose

When struggling to find your life's purpose, remember that each one of us has our own unique gifts. Do not focus on someone else's gifts and wish they were yours. This keeps you SELF-directed. Reach inside and discover your own gifts and reflect them out.

Honor yourself in every way. Wake up and thank the universe for the gift of your breath and the abundance you have whether it be in material possessions or in other unacknowledged richness in your life.

Spend time contemplating your mission here. It is different than someone else's mission. Contemplate the path of your life and all those you have met along the way and all of the messages that have been brought to you. What have you done with those messages? If you ponder long enough, you will discover where your true gifts lie. Through this you will discover your own unique purpose.

Relationships

When seeking a relationship, come to the table with your whole self. Do not enter into a relationship seeking wholeness from the other person. No one can complete you. You must complete yourself first. Balance the triangle of mind, body, and spirit.

Mend your relationship with yourself. Contemplate where you are not whole. Contemplate where you are not Love. Contemplate the reasons why. Dig deep. Study all the patterns that you have learned. These are someone else's belief systems.

Attend to those areas. Disengage from those patterns. Then you can manifest a healthy relationship.

Today

Today is all we have. What if just for today, for just one hour, just one minute, or second, you did something for someone else with no ego centered agenda? If you did this at your expense, whether it be monetary or perhaps physically or otherwise uncomfortable, it would shift the subtle vibrations and lift us all up. We do not know when we will be called home. This ostensibly could be your last act. Make it a loving one and you will leave here with no regrets. Open your heart and live fully today.

Laughter

With global conflict staring us in the face, what is it that we can do to maintain balance and harmony in our daily lives? We have no control over this escalating violence. To a certain degree we do have control over our daily lives. We do have control over how we act or react. Breathe. Just breathe.

And laugh. Deeply laugh. We must keep our sense of humor. Laughter has a healing vibration that uplifts us all. It goes out not only to the planet, but also to the entire universe and envelopes us all in a loving embrace.

Try not to get bogged down in your own daily conflicts. Find the humor in all. It's there if you look hard enough.

Flow Of Abundance

When we define ourselves by our material possessions, we block the flow of abundance. We are more than pieces of paper and material things. To open the flow of abundance, start by being grateful for the abundance you already have. Stop defining yourselves by things that have no real value. It is only the illusion of value that you have been defining yourselves by. Start defining yourselves by what is inside rather than out. In this way you open a channel for abundance to flow freely to you.

"And so you see you need to just go gently with the flow; let the river guide you tenderly to the places you will know." © Dyan Garris 1993-2007. *Voice of the Angels – A Healing Journey Spiritual Cards, The River* card.

Peace

You've undoubtedly heard that laughter is contagious. This is because vibrations such as love, peace, laughter, etc. have a ripple effect. They do reach out and affect others.

If you are constantly in a state of fear, worry or anxiety, this is the vibration you are sending forth into the world. We are not alone. We are all connected. What we do as individuals affects us all on a collective level.

The turmoil in the world seems out of control. It is disturbing to us on a deep level. We feel helpless to do anything to change it. It seems to have a life of its own and it does because we are constantly feeding it.

There is one very simple thing we can do about this. We can begin by making ourselves more peaceful. There is a great deal of power in this very simple thing.

Make peace with everyone in your life that you are at odds with. Make peace with yourself, your boss, your co-worker, your spouse, your ex, your children, your neighbor, your so called mistakes, and your incarnation.

Love yourselves and others and be grateful for the simple yet powerful gift of breath. If we all did this collectively, the Earth itself would breathe a huge sigh of relief. Peace be with all of you today.

Honoring In Relationships

Study all of your connections, all of your relationships. How many of these do you take for granted? How many of these do you not honor in any way? Even a simple "thank you" for a person who nourishes you in some way, even if they are a stranger, is better than nothing at all. There is too much focus on self. Honor everyone that touches your life today in some small way.

Try It On

We sometimes try on energy (relationships, etc.) as we try on sweaters or suits. Some fit and some don't. What matters is whether you hang things back on the hanger or throw them on the floor for someone else to pick up later.

Inadequacy

We do not initially come into the world with a perception of inadequacy. Quite the contrary, we come in innocent and completely lovable. So what happened along the path to make us suspect that we are not quite up to par? Other people's belief systems and other people's patterns were taught to us. That is what happened. Somewhere along the journey we became victims of victims. This is something we can change.

Do everything with your whole self. Do everything from a loving place in your heart. Do your best in every situation. Do not fret that you are not coming up to some impossible or unattainable bar. Reclaim your sense of humor and learn to laugh at yourself and love yourself, even with all of your quirks, instead of crying about not being good enough.

This is a misperception that keeps you locked in a jail of someone else's belief systems and keeps you focused on self, instead of shining out your love and light upon the world. You are perfect the way you are.

Joy and Happiness

Joy and happiness are not goals to look forward to sometime in the future. They are present every day of your life. Add together all your single moments of joy in your life and there is your happiness.

Happiness

When we get a new car, house, boyfriend, girlfriend, partner, spouse, or something we've wanted for a long time, we expect this will make us happy. And for a while perhaps we do have the illusion of being happy, or we do feel pleasure regarding such.

Then later we find that the new house, car, boyfriend, etc. didn't really solve any deep issue within us. It didn't truly make us happy and we wonder why.

When we expect that a person or thing, or anything from the outside, will make us happy, we are giving our power away to that person or thing. These things don't ultimately make us happy because they really only serve to temporarily distract us from whatever our real issues are.

To find true happiness we must first make ourselves happy from the inside. Go inside and discover what it is you are truly plugged into. Discover what it is you truly have your energy invested in. Find all your places that still hurt and heal them through forgiveness. And then happily call your whole spirit back to you. It is then, after becoming complete and whole from the inside, that we begin to attract true happiness on the outside.

Spiritual Math

Give freely of yourself, not because you expect love in return, but because you already have that love to give. In spiritual math, two halves do not necessarily make a whole. One must first make themselves whole and then one will attract the energy they truly desire. We make ourselves whole by knowing where and in what we have our power invested in and by calling our spirits back to us. This is key to manifesting. Thus, the search for our "other half" takes on new meaning.

Tolerance, Compassion, and Breath

Tolerance and compassion for each other must begin somewhere. By beginning on an individual level with something as simple as breathing, we can effect a change and make a difference. Have the courage to try this. For five minutes today, focus on your breathing. Try to connect with all the pain and suffering that is going on in the world. Do this with your breath. Inhale deeply and connect with this. Feel it in your heart. Feel it in every fiber of your being. And then deeply exhale pure compassion and love out into the world. Do this with every fiber of your being. Notice this is not SELF-oriented. Ponder this as you try to see the truth in reducing everything to the bigger picture.

Random Meetings & Chance Encounters

Everything has a reason. Everything has a purpose. If you miss your train, plane, bus, other connection, it is for a reason. You may not know the reason at the time. If you stop and ponder the mystery, you will find answers. Remember *The Celestine Prophecy*? There is always a message for you in any encounter.

We are all connected. Everyone you meet or encounter on the path is there for a reason. You get to choose what, if anything, you will do about it. By our choices we shape the fabric of our lives. Try to see the bigger picture and honor all of your connections, random, chance, or otherwise.

Random Acts Of Kindness

We've all heard it before. We should engage in random acts of kindness. These have a ripple effect that is mostly unseen in the physical realm, but certainly felt by all on every other level. So why don't we do this more often? Why do we not do this without prompting? Why do we do it only when we think about it? It is because we live mostly in our egos with so much focus on self.

On any given day one is presented with multiple opportunities for these acts. When we let go of ego, these acts happen naturally and without thought. This is the true vibration of love and reverberates like angelic music throughout the entire universe.

Grains Of Sand

Every individual grain of sand on the beach is unique and special. Every grain of sand on the beach is connected to every other grain of sand. Each grain has its own unique purpose. Without each individual grain of sand, there would be no beach. We each make up a part of the fabric of life. Each one of us is as unique as every single grain of sand and just as important to the whole beach. Honor yourself and others.

Being In The Moment

"In this moment. . . I am alive."

We have become so busy running around "living" our lives that we have forgotten what a true gift something as simple as breathing really is. Breath is a gift, but something we often take for granted. The vibratory rate of this planet has accelerated to a frenzied pitch. We have the ability to change and shift that frequency with our collective consciousness. We do that by beginning on an individual level.

When we calm ourselves down, calm our pace down, calm our thoughts down and calm our breathing down, the life breath of our Earth will begin to calm down as well.

While you are struggling so hard to get somewhere, your life has passed you by, moment by moment.

Certainly we all have a few daily moments to focus on the gift of breath and to be truly grateful for every moment of our lives. To do this keeps us in the present moment and that is something to be lived fully and cherished completely. In any moment, it is all there is.

 **Illusions**

How do you know if something is real or not? Sometimes something feels so real and yet it is an illusion, a distortion, so that one can learn certain lessons. Sometimes something feels like an illusion and it is real, but presented that way so that one can learn certain lessons. One must look to the fruits in order to discern the truth.

And always look to the underlying vibration. Is it emanating from Love or is it from ego? The Love vibration is the one true thing. Sometimes stubborn egos along with control issues get in the way of love. Fear blocks love.

Love is the highest and best vibration for all in any situation. Ego is what someone wants. Love means being true to your spirit. Love means to reconcile your spirit with your mind and body. Follow your spirit into the vibration of Love, not the mind or body. Love is a balance of mind, body and spirit. Love means letting go of your ego. If you love something, truly love it, let it go and trust that the highest and best for all will occur.

 **Illusions**

When you find yourself hanging on to a person, situation, or stubborn point of view, study what it is that you are really hanging on to and why. Find the underlying issue, whether it is control, fear, etc. If you look hard enough, you will certainly find that whatever it is it is not about Love. When we are not coming from a place of Love, we are not living in the truth; and if we are not living in the truth, then we are living in illusion. The power is in the Love.

Balance

Balance is the perfect equilibrium between mind, body and spirit. Balance begins with our thoughts. Our thoughts then control the body. The body will simply follow suit with whatever thoughts you are feeding it. The spirit will then follow or try to follow with what the body and mind are doing.

Imbalance occurs when one is constantly feeding one's body negative thought patterns. The body becomes unhealthy and the indwelling spirit becomes agitated. Thus we have effectively created imbalance.

How powerful our means to create!

Victim Energy

Why do some people hang on to their patterns of illness? It is because they still serve them in some way. Some people find they get sympathy or other attention for their ailments and so continue to be sick. Sometimes this sympathy or attention is mistaken for love. In reality it is allowing oneself to be a victim.

We must love ourselves completely, wholly, and unconditionally. That means giving up patterns of illness that continue to make us into victims. These patterns are places where we have not or do not love ourselves unconditionally.

If you really study these patterns, you may find that these are something that someone in your tribe or family taught you. Try to see the reflection there. These are someone else's belief systems. At any time you choose, you can eliminate these victim patterns and take all of your power back.

Children

Children are a gift to us. So why sometimes do they aggravate us so much? We expect when we have them that they will be a perfect or higher reflection of ourselves. This is not so. That is our ego's idea of how they should be. In truth, they are a perfect reflection of whatever lessons they came here to learn. They each arrive with their own journey, just as you do.

Give them space and time to be whoever they are. You can guide them on their way; but ultimately you must respect their journey, even if it is not the journey you would choose for them. Each soul has its own unique journey and its own path to follow.

If they disappoint you, forgive them. If they make great accomplishments, exalt in that. Enjoy them in every way you can, not as reflections of yourselves but as their own perfect reflections of God made manifest in the world.

Control

The truth is we don't have much, if any. What we do have is control of our breath. A basic principle of yoga is that while you are in some crazy, contorted and perhaps imperfect pose, you still have control of your breath and you let the rest go. You do what you can do and that's it. It is practice for daily life. Remember this as you go through your stressful day. Just get in your raft and travel to where you are supposed to go. The raft doesn't have any oars, but it is perfectly safe and secure. So relax, float, trust, and breathe.

"A raft is here for traveling on to places yet unknown, so surrender now to love and light and see how much you've grown." © Dyan Garris 1993-2007. *Voice of the Angels – A Healing Journey Spiritual Cards, The Raft* card.

Patterns

We move forward on the path of spiritual growth and transformation by having the courage to change our patterns. These patterns are something that someone has taught us or we have taught ourselves along the way. They are learned behaviors and therefore can be changed.

Usually these patterns are places where we are not being true to ourselves. This is why the universe will give us people, places, and opportunities to change them. It is our free will choice as to what, if anything, we will do about it.

The first step in changing any behavior is to first become aware of it. From there you can decide if it still serves you or not. If it doesn't, eliminate it. Begin by eliminating the underlying need for the pattern.

In order to do that, one must stand completely in their truth. We do a lot of fooling of ourselves, a lot of not loving ourselves; and we make a lot of excuses.

How can anyone else love you in a truly healthy way if you do not first love yourself?

So first identify the places where you are not true to yourself and go forward from there. Then gather your courage for the next part of the journey.

Fabric

Thoughts create the fabric of our lives. We can change our fabric by changing the threads, i.e., changing our thoughts. Be aware of the continual dialogue going on in your mind on a daily basis. Be cognizant of every thought. Whatever you're thinking is what you are creating, and then you live what you've created. Form follows thought.

You might be surprised at what is really going on in your head when you become consciously aware of it. If you find yourself constantly feeding yourself unhealthy thoughts, you can change that. It's like feeding yourself unhealthy food. You can change that pattern by eliminating or adding certain ingredients.

And remember, since we are all connected, whether you realize it or not your thoughts and their associated feelings do go out into the ethers and affect others as well.

So, we do have the ability to change our entire fabric by choosing which threads we will use. While denim and burlap have their good uses, a softer fabric feels better and more soothing against the skin.

Health

What is health anyway? It is simply a perfect equilibrium between mind, body, and spirit. Think of it as an equilateral triangle. It sounds so simple and it is. It is perhaps not easy to achieve for some. Some simply don't achieve health because their illnesses somehow still serve them in some way. Often that is a learned pattern that can be changed or shifted.

Some things that stand in the way of complete health include fretting, worrying, or obsessing about things we cannot change, being unforgiving, hanging on to past hurts and burying them deep inside. These are things that have the frequency to make us ill on a physical level.

Keeping the same thought patterns that you had years ago keeps pain in your body. One must release the past in order to move forward.

Perfect health does not just happen. One must work to make it happen. One must make time for oneself every single day, even if it is only a very few minutes. Your life is a gift. Reflect upon that every day, even on the more challenging days. Remember, we are a product of our choices. We can balance that triangle if we choose.

Abundance

We pray or wish for abundance, all the while not even seeing, recognizing or appreciating the abundance that we already do have. And so we pray and wish and manifest for more, more, more. And then we wonder why things don't show up the way we want them to or in our self-directed time frame. We assume our prayers were not answered or our manifesting did not work.

It is then we sometimes seek counsel from the outside to hopefully hear what we want to hear. Truly such answers lie inside each of us.

In some area of your life you already have abundance. Think about this for a moment. It bears repeating. *In some area of your life you already have abundance.* Identify these areas, honor this existing abundance, and be humbly grateful. In this way, you open a channel for the more, more, more, which you seek, to flow freely to you.

Love

If you had only one day to live, what would you be doing and thinking about? Would you be focusing on business, work, or bills? Would you be dwelling on things or events from the past or people you resent, detest or even hate?

If you had one day to live, your thoughts would probably be centered on thinking about love, people you have loved, and all of the loving moments in your life. You would probably honor and love yourself that last day by doing something you enjoy.

It is interesting to note that usually the last words spoken and the last thoughts of someone facing imminent death are about love. We come in with nothing. We leave with nothing. We create everything in-between. Did you create love in your life?

All healing is self-healing. Does that imply if you are sick that you made yourself so?

Perhaps. We do create with our thoughts, which we can change. We are taught our belief systems, which we can accept or reject. However some do incarnate here as "sick" to teach about the power of Love. So for example, those of you who have innocent, sick children know that this is a lesson in Love. Honor it as such.

Now in terms of illness as a way of being . . . some do use illness as a misguided way to receive love and attention. We will call it, "victimology." Mostly that is just a learned pattern. A learned pattern can be changed. In order to not be a victim, we must do every single thing in our lives from a place of loving intention.

If you resent doing something, you make yourself into a victim.

If you feel that others do not honor or appreciate you, first honor and appreciate yourself. This is the place where healing begins.

I AM Grateful

Realize that while you may perceive someone to have more money or more stuff than you do, you do not have the entire picture. What you have is a perception. You do not really know what someone has gone through to get these material possessions. You do not know what they have given up to get to where you perceive they are in life. You do not know the lessons they have learned on the way to this perceived station in life.

There are a lot of reasons why someone may have more earthly possessions than you. Some have more money or possessions than others simply to teach them that having these things does not speak to the character of a person. Some have these things to teach them the fleeting nature of such material things. Some have more simply to teach them that the true definition of themselves or their self-worth cannot be measured by the amount of stuff they have acquired. In truth, these things are meaningless.

There will always be someone who has more than you do. The natural tendency is to be jealous. When we are jealous, love cannot get through because this is an ego centered position. To return to a heart centered position, simply be grateful and give thanks for all that you do have. If you take a moment to do that, you will see how quickly that brings you back to your true self and how quickly that restores the flow of Love.

Forgiveness

It seems such a simple thing to forgive and yet we sometimes find it such an insurmountable task. We often struggle for quite a long while with forgiving someone then finally we manage to do it. Or so we think. We know we should forgive. We feel we should and so we do and then we wonder why nothing has seemed to change or shift. Why do we not feel better?

The answer is simple. We have forgiven with our linear mind and from a place of ego. We have forgotten to forgive in spirit. It is like doing half the job.

It is easy to forgive in sprit. One must first let go of the ego state of being and enter into a meditative state. Focus on your breathing and follow the breath in and out of your body for a few moments. Breathe slowly, deeply, and evenly. When ready, call the other person's spirit to you. See, feel, know, or visualize their spirit right before you.

See, feel, know or visualize the angry red cords that still bind the two of you to this particular karma. Say or communicate to this person's spirit that you wish to forgive them. See, feel, know, or visualize the communication entering that person's energy field. See them accepting the communication of forgiveness.

Then thank the person for this lesson, bless them and release them. Now simply erase, remove, or unplug the angry cord or cords that connect the two of you to this karma.

Then watch what happens. Return slowly to your physical awareness feeling wonderfully free and empowered.

Forgiveness

Being stuck in our perceptions is what keeps us from moving forward. If you perceive that someone has hurt you or wronged you in some way, be aware that they may have the same perception of you. You may not realize that. That puts you at a stalemate where no progress can be made if someone does not make the first move toward forgiveness. This is how divorce happens. This is how wars start. Take a small step toward forgiveness and see what happens.

Tale of Woe

Life here is a series of choices. We make our choices and then we live with the consequences of whatever we have created. If you find yourself saying, "I can't," because of some imagined limitation that comes from someone or somewhere else, you must learn to take responsibility for the co-creation of that current reality. If you find you have a "tale of woe," go back and study the origins of that "woe." Once you see your part in the creation of it, you can begin to effect a change, if that is not what you desire to create. To do otherwise keeps you in a victim role. And truly, no one can keep you as a victim unless you allow it to be so. So if you feel that you have limitations, look to where you have created the illusion of such and why.

Study and eliminate the patterns that came from your previous connections. This does not happen overnight. We do it moment by moment. Life truly is a healing journey; and if we reflect deeply enough upon it and begin to see how everything and everyone is connected by the threads of the blanket of life, miracles can occur.

Fish Tale Of Woe – Lost At Sea

Let's say you are sitting in the middle of the ocean in a small boat. Your boat springs a slow leak. You pray for someone to come and save you. Soon, along comes a larger boat. By this time you are really thirsty. The people in the larger boat offer to throw you a towline. You are focused on your thirst; so you tell them you are just thirsty and could use some water. *If only you had some water!*

They throw you some ice cold bottled water. They ask again if they can throw you a lifeline. There may be some work involved with this, i.e., you may have to stand up and actually attach the line to your own boat and do a few other things.

Plus, you really are afraid of falling out of your boat and maybe even losing your very attractive and expensive sunglasses in the process. Your thirst quenched, you decline the lifeline, content to wait for someone to save you. They move along their path.

Pretty soon your slow leak is getting larger and a storm is coming. You pray again for someone to come and save you. Along comes another larger boat. By this time you are really hungry, and this is a fishing boat on its way in with its big catch of the day. They offer you a lifeline. You see the fruits of their all day labor and you want this for yourself.

You feel entitled because, after all, you are in a leaky boat and they have a bigger boat. You say, "If only I had some fish I wouldn't be hungry anymore."

So they throw you some fish, which you gobble up. It's free. It's fresh. And it's good! They again offer you a lifeline. Your stomach full, you politely decline because now you are a bit too satiated and sleepy to do whatever is required to tow your boat in. You don't even really care anymore. *That fish was really good!* Your boat seems comfortable enough for now; and eventually someone will come along and save you. They depart.

Your boat soon starts sinking; and while it is going down you wonder why no one showed up to save you. You go down thinking, as you always have, that this kind of stuff always happens to you.

What is it with this feeling of entitlement? What is it with the idea that someone is going to save you or that saving you is a "miracle?" This is not a miracle. No one is going to save you. People may offer you assistance, but you have to actually do something to assist yourself as well.

Even if you are afraid to reach over and tie the lifeline to your boat, or do whatever else may be necessary to assist in your "saving," it is better to try to do so than to sink and drown, all the while wondering what in the world happened.

There are those that truly would go down saying to themselves that at least someone thought enough of them to give them basics such as food and water. Did you perhaps forget to think enough of yourself to provide yourself with such?

And there are those who would go down blaming their parents or someone else for not providing them with swimming lessons!

There are many who are willing to provide you with basics. You may not even appreciate those basics or those foundations until you have to provide them for yourself. You may not even realize you have been provided with basics on which and with which to build a foundation. But know this: You are not entitled to have anyone else provide them for you, unless you are an infant or minor child.

Is it necessary to take things in your life to the point where you are actually sitting in a teensy little boat with a hole in it in the middle of the ocean before you realize that you are not entitled to have a bigger, better boat just because?

Grow up. Take responsibility; grab some oars and maybe some plumber's putty and some other tools before you embark on your journey.

And perhaps somewhere on your voyage (which ostensibly will be farther then) you will figure out how to honorably procure a larger, more seaworthy craft for your travels if that is what you desire.

Fish Tale Of Woe – Lost At Sea Part II

So, to continue our fish tale. . . Before your boat sinks completely, another even larger boat comes by and offers you a towline. This time you take it. You even manage to tie the rope to your boat all by yourself without falling in, however you do lose your designer sunglasses and woefully, the money you had in your pockets did fall into the ocean and got washed away.

When you safely reach shore, the captain of the larger boat bids you farewell with a wave and a smile. You do not offer to exchange anything with this captain or crew because your money was lost at sea and it doesn't occur to you to offer anything else. Plus, you feel entitled to be "saved," primarily because you were sinking; and after all, you are the one with the smaller boat.

In any event, you are now safe. You are on your own. You are free from impending doom; but you are not free from your patterns yet, as we shall see. You notice an older building with a sign in the window that says:

Before we get to that however, there are some things you do not see because you only have your own limited perspectives. The larger boat was taking a risk by towing you in. They ended up having to get new engines and repairing some other general damage that occurred by the towing of your boat. The captain also paid his crew overtime for their extra time and effort.

You, of course, will never come to find this out; and even if you did find out, you would have zero intention of doing anything about it (what could you even *do*?!) because you wouldn't consider it to be your issue. The captain can afford to fix these things himself – look at the size of his boat! And his crew is his responsibility.

"The ocean can be moody, but full of life then too; let the healing power that's there now gently enter you." © Dyan Garris 1993-2007. *Voice of the Angels – A Healing Journey Spiritual Cards, The Ocean* card.

Now on with the story. . .

Fish Tale Of Woe – Lost At Sea Part III

You walk into the building with the sign in the window. You are darn thirsty again and you could really use a cigarette after all you've been through. *My God, what an ordeal you've endured!* And you still have the challenge of getting your boat fixed so you can continue on your journey.

The building is a bar/restaurant with a lot of local flavor. *Wonderful!* Come to think of it, you could really use a drink. How convenient. But you have no money since all of your pieces of paper got washed away when you helped tie the towrope to your boat.

You sidle up to the bar and pitifully explain your tale of woe to the bartender. You even shed a tear or two for all you've been through.

Feeling sorry for you, as you had hoped, the bartender pours you a stiff one and says it's on the house. *Excellent!* You gratefully gulp it down. You bum a cigarette from a patron. The bar is filled with people and you are hoping someone will take pity upon you and your recent travails and buy you another drink.

No one does, however, even though you are freely and happily exchanging tales of woe and fish tales with whomever is in earshot. You have always understood the reciprocal language of victim-speak. But what you fail to realize is that these are fishermen/women. They work and they work hard. They are really victims to nothing and they truly do not understand your language.

After relating your tale of woe to many in hope that someone will help you out here, someone mentions that help is wanted at this establishment. They need a dishwasher. You are astounded at this suggestion. *This work is completely beneath you! You cannot possibly do such a thing!*

You may have a small, leaky boat; but you have an education. You have a Ph.D. You even have five courses of mathematics! You mention this to someone, even though they are not particularly impressed. Theirs is a different world in which pieces of paper as definitions of who you are really do not matter much. But in your "real world" you are a very big and important person. *No, you cannot even consider such a thing as being a dishwasher!*

Do we all know someone like this? You aren't like this, are you? This story is about entitlement, victim-speak, manipulation, perspectives, limited viewpoints and more.

Fish Tale Of Woe – Lost At Sea Part IV

You decide that you better get out of this place fast before the natives get restless. *Truly!* You need to find someone real to help you fix your boat so you can get out of here. You silently curse that captain. *What was he thinking bringing you here?*

You exit the bar/restaurant and start walking. You're just sort of meandering around, but what a hike it is! You see a sign that says:

Healer/Priest/Priestess This Way ➜

You follow the arrow. Certainly the Healer will help you get out of here.

You walk on an uphill path in the direction of the arrow, thinking to yourself this Healer better be worth it.

You soon come to a clearing and you see a big, beautiful dwelling. You think to yourself that this Healer must be very rich and powerful and certainly in a good position to help you. *For Free*, of course. Isn't "healing" always free? Aren't these people just doing what they are supposed to be doing? Isn't Spirituality free? *"Yes,"* you say to yourself, *"Of course it is!"*

You come upon a big carved wooden door. This is really ornate. You reiterate to yourself, "My, this person must be really well compensated."

You knock on door with the very expensive looking doorknocker. *Very impressive!* You expect a servant to answer, but after a brief wait the Healer/Priest/Priestess answers personally instead.

 **Fish Tale Of Woe – Lost At Sea Part V**

Now what good story does not include a flashback?

Let's rewind a little. After you leave the bar/restaurant, you are followed by a pack of angry looking canines. You are afraid of dogs because as a child you were mauled by one and almost blinded in the process. This has traumatized you for life. You do not like dogs. Why are these things following you? *And curses on that captain again for bringing you here!*

You walk on hoping they will just go away. This can't possibly happen to you again, can it? But they don't go away and the more fearful you become, the more aggressive they seem to become. You are attracting this to you by your fear, but you wouldn't quite put it that way. You just want them to leave you alone. But, as I said, they don't.

To your horror, you actually do end up getting attacked by these nasty looking creatures; and this is why you are overjoyed, albeit torn and tattered, at finally arriving at and knocking on the very ornate and impressive door of the Healer. This person is meant to help you!

Open up already! You are wounded!

Fish Tale Of Woe – Lost at Sea Part VI

The door is answered by the Healer. From now on we will refer to this person as "HPP." "Wow," you think to yourself. "I want whatever this person is having." Your wounded gaze is met by the deepest, clearest, most aquamarine eyes you have ever seen. Come to think of it, you don't recall seeing eyes this color ever before. You are temporarily mesmerized.

You manage to snap out of it and gather your wits. You don't know what's wrong with you. You normally have legendary cool. "I'm wounded!" you exclaim in case HPP didn't hear you yelling when you were outside the door. You look behind you and the dogs have thankfully disappeared.

HPP gazes upon you lovingly and beckons you in. "Ah, yes," HPP says. "Being one of the keepers of the sacred records, I've been expecting you. You're a little early, but I saw you in my crystal ball not too long ago. Come, I've made you some pancakes."

You'll have pancakes as long as they're free you think to yourself. Judging by the looks of this place, they can't be free. You have no money, after all. What does this person expect from you? You're a little wary and all you want is healing. *That has got to be free!*

You cautiously follow along behind HPP down a long corridor, dripping a conspicuous trail of blood on the marble floor. You begin to wonder if this person knows what they are doing. They seem a bit daft. HPP doesn't even seem to notice the blood.

Still, you find yourself strangely attracted or drawn to this person in some odd way. It feels like you've known one another forever. This makes you feel a bit uncomfortable, but you'll go along with it for now. *You need healing!*

You take a seat at an ornately carved alder table. *Impressive.* As you wait patiently for your pancakes and maybe a bandage or two, you look around. You notice many crystals, gemstones, and some items you don't recognize. You make a somewhat subconscious note of the gemstones.

HPP brings you some bandages and tends to your flesh wounds. *Finally!* Soon after that a plate of steaming pancakes appears on the table seemingly out of thin air. You must have lost more blood than you thought. You're imagining things.

You wolf them down. *Not bad.* You're hungry and exhausted after your ordeal. Yes, these are free, you've decided. HPP has more than enough of everything!

Fish Tale Of Woe – Lost At Sea Part VII

All in all, you spend a total of six months with HPP. HPP tends to your wounds and makes you feel better. Physically, you are pain free for the first time in your life. One day HPP tells you that it is time to embark upon a vision quest. For this you will need to learn to breathe in a certain way. You practice that, endlessly it seems. Then suddenly the day of travel is upon you.

HPP and you go on your trip and hike for what seems to be forever. After much ado, you end up on a very high bluff. You feel at peace there. You could stay forever. HPP tells you that you are looking for your totem. Suddenly appears a leopard.

HPP informs you that this is your totem. You seem to get a sense of the truth of that. You accept, in some way, but you have no idea what this totem represents or even what a totem is.

Nor do you much care, actually. You find that your needs in the moment are being met and that is all that matters to you. HPP takes care of your physical pain and most of all your other needs as well.

You have an uneasy feeling about the ultimate tab here, but you remind yourself that this is all free. You don't give much deep thought to the leopard and eventually it disappears.

Upon returning from your travels and to the main house, you dream several times about the leopard. You still have no idea what any of that means and no cause to delve deeper.

Somewhere along the line it becomes clear that your flesh wounds are attended to, and spiritually you have gone as far as you are willing to go here.

It is clear that it is time to move along the path. Because HPP does not feel you have learned all you have come to learn he/she is sad, but also accepts that it is time for you to go. You say your goodbyes to each other, however inept and however untimely.

On your way out, you find a check at the door. It is made out to you and is drawn on *The First National Bank of Karma*. The amount is for $3,765.00.

So thinking that it belongs to you, primarily because it has your name on it, you pocket it. This will come in handy.

You walk down to the shore. You do not get attacked by dogs again. The way is smooth. You are self-satisfied; and you take it as a sign, thinking that you have indeed learned something from your time with HPP.

You eventually find your boat where you left it. Your trust in the innate goodness of the human race renews.

You see that the boat still has a hole in it. You idly wonder why some native did not fix it for you in your absence. You check your pockets to see what you could possibly use to plug it up.

You just want to get back to where you were. You've learned a lot; but *thank you very much,* you just want to be on your way home.

The only thing you have in your pockets is that check. You consider for a few moments. It is the only thing that may get you out of here. You decide to use it to try to plug the hole. You push it in there and to your surprise you find that it works!

The check turns into a rubbery substance, expands into the hole, and seems to be working quite nicely. *Very good!* You shove off back into the ocean and back to where you came from. You just want to get home. Yes, you learned something! *It didn't cost you anything at all.*

On your third day at sea, your boat springs a leak. The check has run out or perhaps it has bounced.

You find yourself once again sitting in the middle of the ocean in a boat with a hole in it. A storm is coming again. The boat is sinking.

Along comes another bigger boat. It is that same captain that originally towed you in. He asks if you want a tow. You tell him yes, but please not to the same place.

He obliges and you find yourself once again tying the line he throws you to your end of the boat. This time you have nothing to lose. There is nothing left to fall into the raging sea. *Woe is you!*

And this time things are different. He does not take you to the same island. He instead invites you onto his boat. You accept, leaving your own boat tossing violently in the erratic sea.

You climb aboard and the captain takes you into his chambers. Inside is a leopard.

You cautiously keep your distance, never understanding what the leopard was about anyway.

Uneasily, you broach the subject. You tell the captain you just want to get home. The captain tells you that you are home. *What?!* You tell him you do not understand and you are unwilling to put up with any more drama or nonsense or things you do not understand.

You went through this crazy motion. In the process you lost your money in the sea; you lost a check for $3,765.00. And you remind him that you lost your designer sunglasses as well. You did everything that was asked or expected of you, did you not?

The captain looks at you with sadness in his eyes and tries to explain.

"My child," He says. "The very first time that you chose to refuse help and your boat went down is when you died.

"When we came along and offered you a tow, you were already gone.

"We took you to a place where you had a chance of life anew. And there you applied all of your old thinking and all of your old patterns to a new situation.

"You learned absolutely nothing new, and in fact incurred new karma by taking something that appeared to be yours but was not. In this world things are not always what they seem.

"You cannot go back. You can only go forward. The leopard is to remind you that leopards do not change their spots. You did not accept the leopard as your totem because you refused to see your unwillingness to change. You refused to see your part in your own incarnation. You refused to take responsibility.

"But, one can choose a different animal as a totem at the appropriate time. You and the animal will choose each other.

"Now this incarnation is over, but I will take you to the place where you can start over. You will not remember any of this on a conscious level, but you will have signals and you will meet people that remind you in some way of the life lessons that you are supposed to learn. These people and things will seem vaguely familiar to you.

"You will even encounter a leopard and will again have a choice about whether or not to accept the learning of this totem into your life or not. It is up to you.

"You can also choose, as you had a choice whether or not to accept a towline or to take the check or not, to look at this incarnation as a complete failure or as something that impacts you and others on a universal level. It is your choice whether or not to accept this lifetime as a failure or as a success.

"Those reading your story now may come to understand the role they play in their own fish tale. They also have the choice as you did as to whether or not their story becomes a tale of woe or not. It is all a choice."

And with that, life began anew.

"The End." Or, depending upon your point of view, "The Beginning."

The Recipe Of Life

Life is like a recipe. You assemble your ingredients and then mix them up and hopefully come out with something palatable. You can make yourself something barely passable, or you can make yourself a veritable feast. You decide how much time and effort you want to put in. Remember that you are the head chef in this particular recipe.

The Ability To Create

Trust in your ability to create. You have the ability to create a flowing stream of income. You have the ability to create whatever you desire. You just forgot. Sometimes you need someone to remind you and that is where psychic readings come in, although, as we said, you already know this. A psychic reading is perhaps just a reminder.

Resolve

Now is a good time to resolve old issues. Let the emotions come up to the surface and bubble out. From there the slate can be cleared.

How many are harboring resentment, jealousy, and/or harsh feelings toward a family member, old friend, or someone that you used to be close to? Clearing these things up may seem like an unpleasant task.

However, it doesn't have to be if egos can be moved aside long enough to speak to the person's spirit, rather than their earthly distortion, or your distortion of how you think they really are.

Let go of what you think the person is about long enough to learn something valuable. Usually when such deep feelings are involved, you can be assured that whatever it is relates to some sort of important life lesson. You can avoid whomever or whatever all you want.

However, since it is a life lesson, you will repeat it over and over with others in one form or another until you learn it. Patterns repeat. Avoidance is only temporary and you can fool yourself into thinking it works if you want. It's better to resolve it. (Or re-solve). Do you see?

Wake Up Call

If you awakened to seeing everyone as a soul instead of a body, would that change your thoughts and actions? If you awakened to the fact that everything is a lesson in Love and that we're all presenting each other with opportunities to learn about Love and become that Love, would that change your thoughts and actions? If you awakened to the higher purpose of everything, would that change your thoughts and actions?

Everything you are presented with and everyone you meet has a purpose. That purpose is to help you love. It is when you are so far removed from the truth of

194

who you really are and so caught up in illusions of duality consciousness that you cannot even begin to see the truth. Wake up, open your eyes, and really see.

Missing

There are a few things you should know about missing someone. Perhaps you don't really miss them and whatever unpleasantness or pleasantness you once shared. What you are missing is their spirit and the idea of them. Your spirit remembers the love.

You are missing their essence and not the earthly distortion. Knowing that, you should also know that if you were once that close you were always that close – in spirit – and therefore, there is nothing to miss. They are a permanent part of you and are always there in your heart.

In this illusion that we live in, it may appear that they are gone. Or your relationship may be temporarily distorted, because you agreed somewhere along the line to teach each other lessons. But again, they are not gone. They are still with you. There is nothing to miss. Celebrate that knowledge as truth.

Gratitude

There is so much that so many of us take for granted. Spending a few minutes a day in the loving space of gratitude raises and shifts the vibration not only of your personal realm but has a global impact as well. Try to remember who you are, why you came here, and what you're really about without all of the drama and illusion. Step fully into the light and wholeheartedly embrace your incarnation here as the gift it truly is.

Expansion Bridge

Consciousness expands through the illusion of limitation. It's what you do with that entire illusion that matters. Do you take a chance and cross the bridge, or do you cower in fear and stay where you are wondering why your life isn't changing?

"All bridges are but connections to where you need to go; they are the link between where you are and what you want to know." © Dyan Garris 1993-2007. *Voice of the Angels – A Healing Journey Spiritual Cards, The Bridge* card.

At The Heart Of The Matter

Whenever we are emotionally invested in something, be it relationship, job, or other, we have a tendency to not really see what is going on. We'll feel whatever it is, be it "good" or "bad", in our bodies before we ever see it. It is easier for someone else to see your situation more clearly than you do while you're in it.

Now, for those involved in stressful situations and staying in them, ask yourself why. I can guarantee you that at the heart of that answer is because of a pattern. You stay because you are engaging in some sort of pattern that you learned somewhere – either in childhood or elsewhere. In order to change a pattern, one must first really see it and then be willing to do something about it.

Figure out the pattern and you can then figure out what to do. If you don't get rid of the pattern, you will continue to encounter lessons that challenge you to do so. So, you can leave the person, job, situation, etc.; but at some point you must directly address the pattern. It's at the heart.

The Boss

If you are asking, "When," you are not living in the present moment. If you're not living in the present moment, you're missing the point of your life. If you are asking, "How," you are blocking the universe's ability to bring you that which you desire. Nothing can occur until you stop trying to tell the universe what to do and when to do it. So those praying for miracles, unless you know how to perform them, step aside and see what happens.

Transition

Transition seems difficult because we are often unwilling or unable to give up our patterns. But we must move forward no matter how uncomfortable. Nothing stays static. So have the courage to walk through the fire. Your feet may feel burned; but ultimately they will emerge tougher and stronger and therefore will be able to take your farther on your journey.

Transition

Transition is that noisy, crowded and perhaps uncomfortable train station where everyone else seems to know which train to get aboard. Just know that after you get your bearings, you'll be able to figure that out too. In the meantime, there are two rules: (1) Don't hop aboard the first train that comes by just to be going somewhere and (2) Don't let anyone push you onto the tracks.

Where AM I?

Our capacity to love is reborn over and over again through the illusion of challenge. Without challenge how do we remember who we are? Life here would be flat and boring and pointless. Do not underestimate your ability to rise above every challenge. This is where you rediscover yourself.

"The sun that's rising slowly is but a glimmer of what's to be. So know that as you go along now; we are here with thee." © Dyan Garris 1993-2007. *Voice of the Angels – A Healing Journey Spiritual Cards, The Island – Sunrise* card.

"The sun that's setting slowly is but a glimmer of what's to be. So know that as you go along; an ending is a beginning for thee." © Dyan Garris 1993-2007. *Voice of the Angels – A Healing Journey Spiritual Cards, The Island – Sunset* card.

Other Products Available By This Author

Voice of the Angels – A Healing Journey
Spiritual Cards
by Dyan Garris

A beautiful thirty card deck based on scenes from the guided fantasy *A Healing Journey*. Each card has its own special channeled message in rhythmic quatrain verse from the angels. The box of cards includes a 67 page instruction booklet showing twelve ways to lay out the cards, *Transformational Healing Exercise*, healing affirmations, and more. These cards were not computer generated and therefore have different core energy than similar decks. Real crystals and other elements were used to create the cards. A journal is available separately. Use for spiritual growth, divination and spiritual transformation.

The Journal

Voice of the Angels Cookbook
Talk To Your Food! – Intuitive Cooking
by Dyan Garris

This is an adventure in opening the creative centers and communicating with your food so that it can transform from raw ingredients into what truly nourishes you on every level. The book includes twelve food related channeled messages, several "Intuitively Speaking" paragraphs which explain how to prepare the recipe using one's own unique creativity, and sixty full color photographs.

CDs by Dyan Garris

There are six CDs in the series of music and meditation for healing, relaxation, guided meditation, chakra balance, help in sleeping, and vibrational attunement. Each CD consists of six or seven tracks of instrumental music plus a guided meditation on the last track. Titles are: *A Healing Journey – The Voice of the Angels, Moment by Moment – Music For The Soul, Reflection, Patterns, Illusions,* and *Connections.* Each CD vibrates to a specific chakra and each is for a specific purpose.

There are four compilation CDs – two volumes of music only and two volumes of guided meditation only. Music only compilation titles are: *Spiritus Sanctus,* Volume 1 and 2. Guided meditation only compilation titles are: *Perfect Pathways*, Volume 1 and 2.

The CD *Release* is eleven tracks of soothing instrumental relaxation music for those who need a release. The very angelic vocals of award winning recording artist Amber Norgaard can be heard on the songs "Breathe" and "Sleep."

Voice of the Angels Meditation Basket

Meditation Basket

The Meditation Basket includes all six soul soothing CDs in the series of music and guided meditation for self-healing, chakra balancing, relaxation and vibrational attunement by Dyan Garris. The beautiful lined reusable basket comes with an angelic scroll of healing affirmations, authentic and powerful Tibetan meditation crystal, high quality incense and holder, and a clean burning, great smelling Reiki charged meditation candle in its own jar with its own affirmation. Beginner to experienced will find the "Journeys" on the last track of each CD healing and refreshing!

The Meditation Journal

Voice of the Angels Meditation Journal is for recording your meditative journeys. It is designed to be used with the CD series of music and guided meditation by Dyan Garris for self-healing, chakra balance, stress release, help in sleeping, and vibrational attunement of mind, body, and spirit. However, it can be used for recording any meditation journey or nightly dreams. Transformation and deeper levels of learning can be achieved by keeping a record of what transpires in a meditative state. *The Meditation Journal* serves as a helpful and integrative tool between the linear mind and the subconscious, meditative mind.

About The Author
Dyan Garris

For many years, Dyan Garris has been counseling clients in order to help them positively move forward in their lives. She is clairvoyant, clairaudient, and clairsentient. In addition, Dyan is also what is known as a voice recognition psychic and trance channel. This means that she can help her clients via phone, which is how she conducted her readings throughout her career.

Growing up in Illinois, Dyan became aware of her clairvoyance, and other gifts, at a very young age. She spent years learning how to use these gifts to help others.

In 2005 she created a CD series of music and meditation for self-healing, relaxation, chakra balancing, and vibrational attunement.

She is the author, artist, and developer of *Voice of the Angels – A Healing Journey Spiritual Cards.* This is a 30 card deck of divination angel cards based upon scenes from *A Healing Journey – Guided Fantasy,* which is the guided meditation found on the last track of *A Healing Journey – The Voice of the Angels CD.* Each card has its own channeled message in rhythmic quatrain verse from the Angels who are the "voice" in Voice of the Angels.

Her new book, *Voice of the Angels Cookbook – Talk to Your Food! – Intuitive Cooking* is now available at the author's website, www.voiceoftheangels.com and www.amazon.com. This is an adveture in opening the creative centers and communicating with your food so that it can transform from raw ingredients into what truly nourishes you on every level. The book includes twelve food related channeled messages and several "Intuitively Speaking" paragraphs, which explain how to prepare the recipe using one's own unique creativity.

Visit www.voiceoftheangels.com or www.newagecd.com for further information.